FALLINGWATER

Edgar Kaufmann, jr.

Introduction by Mark Girouard

FALLINGWATER
A FRANK LLOYD WRIGHT COUNTRY HOUSE

Principal Photography by Christopher Little and Thomas A. Heinz

Measured Drawings by L. D. Astorino & Associates, Ltd.

ABBEVILLE PRESS PUBLISHERS NEW YORK LONDON

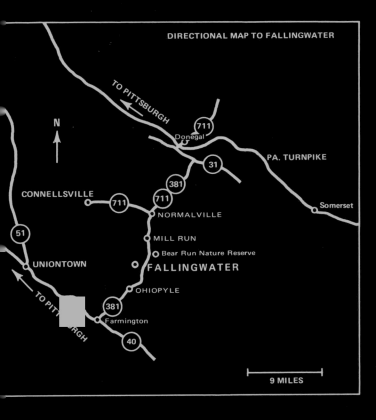

DIRECTIONAL MAP TO FALLINGWATER

9 MILES

Fallingwater telephone: 724-329-8501

EDITOR: Walton Rawls

DESIGNER: Jim Wageman

LIBRARY OF CONGRESS CATALOGING-IN-PUBLIC DATA

Kaufmann Edgar, 1910–1989
    Fallingwater, a Frank Lloyd Wright country house.
    Bibliography: p.
    Includes index.
    1.Wright, Frank LLoyd, 1867–1959—Criticism and
interpretation. 2. Fallingwater (Pa.) 3. Usonian
houses—Pennsylvania. 4. Kaufmann family—Homes and
haunts. Title
NA737.W7K29 1986   728.3'72'0924   86-13967

ISBN-13: 978-0-89659-662-7
ISBN-10: 0-89659-662-1

The quote from Jean-Paul Sartre on page 172 appeared in Adieux
by Simon De Beauvoir (New York: Pantheon, 1982). The quote
from Giambattista Vico on page 183 comes from Scienza Nuova
Seconda (Naples, 1744).

For bulk and premium sales and for text adoption procedures,
write to Customer Service Manager, Abbeville Press, 137 Varick
Street, New York, NY 10013, or call 1-800-ARTBOOK.

Visit us online at www.abbeville.com

CONTENTS

INTRODUCTION

The House and the Natural Landscape: A Prelude to Fallingwater

Drawing by Thomas Hearne of Sir George Beaumont and Joseph Farington sketching a waterfall in the Lake District of England, 1770s.

A charming drawing by Thomas Hearne shows Sir George Beaumont and Joseph Farington sketching a waterfall in the Lake District, sometime in the 1770s. Waterfalls were being visited and sketched all over the British Isles at this period. But although gentlemen of taste sketched waterfalls, they did not build houses by them, still less over them. Nonetheless, a continuous thread connects Sir George Beaumont, sketching his waterfall in the 1770s, to Edgar J. Kaufmann, commissioning Frank Lloyd Wright to build Fallingwater in the 1930s. Between them lies a gradual development of the romantic imagination, and of attitudes to the natural landscape and to the problem of how buildings should, or should not, be fitted into it.

In the eighteenth century, when English travelers first began to appreciate natural scenery, and to tour the mountains, lakes, rocks, waterfalls, and wild places of the British Isles, their attitude was by no means uncritical. For them "nature" was the supreme arbiter, but by "nature" they understood a Platonic ideal that actual natural scenery did not necessarily live up to. They had come to their appreciation by way of art and poetry, and traveled with minds conditioned by the way artists had painted wild landscapes, or poets had written about them, in both cases selecting and adjusting in order to compose a picture or a poem. A guide to the Lake District, first published in 1778, set out to take tourists "from the delicate touches of Claude, verified in Coniston Lake, to the noble scenes of Poussin, exhibited on Windermere-water, and from there to the stupendous romantic ideas of Salvator Rosa, realized in the Lake of Derwent." When looking at a view, travelers would pass judgment on it, and mentally readjust it if necessary.

Scenery was condemned for being too simple or too bare. A landscape of heather and rocks needed trees to break its outlines and give it light and shade. "Mere rocks," wrote Thomas Whately in his *Observations on Modern Gardening* (1770), "may surprise, but can hardly please; they are too far removed from common life, too barren and inhospitable, rather desolate than solitary, and more horrid than terrible." Rocks were improved by water falling over or running through them; this produced a broken light and a broken sound that was both picturesque and pleasing. Trees, rocks, and water joined together in the right proportions made up a picturesque composition.

Conventions developed about what did, or did not, go with particular views or features. Some types of buildings harmonized with waterfalls: Whately, for instance, described with approval "an iron forge, covered with a black cloud of smoke, and surrounded with half-burned ore" next to the "roar of a waterfall" on the River Wye. It suggested "the ideas of force or of danger" and was "perfectly compatible with the wildest romantic situations." But a regular house next to a waterfall was a solecism: it spoiled the picture because it had the wrong associations. Looked at the other way, a wild landscape coming right up to a house spoiled the house. "And while rough thickets shade the lonely glen,/Let culture smile upon the haunts of men," wrote Richard Payne Knight in his poem *The Landscape* (1795). A house of any size needed a park, and a park while it should never be formal, had "a character distinct from a *forest*; for while we admire, and even imitate, the romantic wildness of nature, we ought never to forget that a park is the habitation of men." (Humphry Repton, *An Enquiry into the Changes in Landscape Gardening*, 1806)

So it came about that when eighteenth-century devotees of the picturesque painted or drew "the romantic wildness of nature" they depicted it without domestic accompaniments; when they imitated it, they imitated it out of sight of their houses; and when they went to live in it, they inserted an intermediary zone of culture and cultivation between house and wilderness. Hafod in Wales, for instance, which was the most famous wild demesne in eighteenth-century Britain, was renowned for its waterfalls. But none of these was in sight of the house, which was built in a more pastoral setting of greensward and grazing cattle.

Country-house owners whose property did not happen to contain waterfalls not infrequently constructed an artificial one. At Bowood, in Wiltshire, Lord Shelburne made one at the end of an artificial lake, after the model of a picture by Poussin. Lord Stamford's new cascade at Enville in Staffordshire was described with enthusiasm by Joseph Heely: "I think I never saw so fine an effect from light and shade, as is here produced by the gloom of evergreens and other trees, and the peculiar brightness of the foaming water." (*Letters on the Beauties of Hagley, Envil and the Leasowes,* 1777) But neither fall was in sight of the house. The most that was considered suitable to embellish a waterfall was a statue or inscription, perhaps to a departed relative or friend, suitable to the mood of gentle melancholy induced by the sound of water; or a seat from which to admire it. The latter had to be in the right mode, however, like that at the Leasowes, near Enville: "a rude seat, composed of stone, under rugged roots."

Unlike ordinary houses, castles, especially ruined castles, were also considered appropriate features in wild scenery. They definitely had the right romantic connotations. But sometimes castles were still lived in, and sometimes they needed to be rebuilt. Culzean Castle in Ayrshire, for instance, was an old fortified house on a cliff top overlooking

16

Culzean Castle, in Ayrshire, painted by Alexander Nasmyth in the early 19th century.

Dunglass, in Haddingtonshire, 1807–13.

the sea. Its position was superb, its family associations were valued, but as a house the building failed to meet the late-eighteenth-century standards of accommodation and comfort. Between 1777 and 1792 it was rebuilt to the designs of Robert Adam, but in his own individual version of a castle style, in sympathy with its site. The new house rose straight from the cliffs, like the old one.

Culzean pioneered a fresh approach, based on the idea that the architecture of a new house could be adapted to fit it to a wild situation. In the early nineteenth century a number of such houses were built, on dramatic sites or in wild settings, even when there had been no house there before. Normally they were built in a castle manner, but some, like Dunglass in Haddingtonshire, were built in the classical style, though on an asymmetric plan and with a broken outline, to fit the site. Such houses continued to be built through the nineteenth century. In the 1870s the architect Richard Norman Shaw established his reputation by designing Leyswood in Sussex, and Cragside in Northumberland, on dramatic rocky sites to which the houses played up with fragmented plans, soaring verticals, and picturesquely broken roofs. Shaw was consciously continuing the picturesque tradition, but, on the whole, new houses in this kind of position were built comparatively seldom in the British Isles.

When clients or architects did opt for a wild site it was usually an elevated one, with the house rising out of wild nature rather than melting into it. This was partly because such houses were built for people of position, who wanted their place of residence to have a degree of importance; but also because houses on higher land had a view, and enclosed low-lying situations were thought to be unhealthy. It was probably for these reasons that houses down by waterfalls were a rarity.

There was one building type, however, that could appropriately be designed to melt into its surroundings. This was the cottage. An interest in natural scenery had almost inevitably led to an appreciation of the way in which nature worked on and weathered man-made structures. Ruins appealed to eighteenth-century eyes in part because they were usually overgrown with moss and creepers. Artists on the look-out for picturesque effects also began to take an interest in old cottages, particularly when they were so dilapidated that nature seemed to be taking them over, to the delight of the artist if not of the inhabitants. "Moral and picturesque ideas do not always coincide," as William Gilpin put it. (*Observations on Several Parts of England*, 1808)

From the mid-eighteenth century onward similar effects, suitably adapted to cope with problems of keeping out wind and weather, began to be incorporated into new buildings. Thatched roofs, rough undressed stonework, and creeper-clad porches and verandahs made of untrimmed branches, often with the bark left on them, were especially popular. To begin with these elements were confined to buildings such as grottoes, hermitages, and bathhouses, which were built as features in a park rather than to be lived in. But by the end of the eighteenth century they were being used for residential cottages. These included elaborate "*cottages ornées*," designed for the residence of ladies and gentlemen themselves, especially when they were on holiday by the seaside, or in retreat from the responsibilities of an active life. In such situations dignity and importance were not called for; people went to live in a *cottage ornée* specifically in order to feel that they were escaping from the conventions of society and tasting something of the rural innocence that poets had always associated with cottage life: "the insinuating effusions of the muse, that true happiness is only to be found in a sequestered and rural life," as William Heely put it.

Perhaps the most alluring *cottage ornée* ever built is the so-called Swiss Cottage at Cahir, in southern Ireland. It was designed, possibly by John Nash, for the Earl of Glengall in about 1820. Its position is a singularly beautiful and peaceful one, on a low rise above a reach of the River Suir. The cottage was, and is, almost swallowed up by the woods that envelop it, and by its own thatched roofs and rustic verandahs. Inside, however, a selection of highly fashionable French wallpapers kept Lord Glengall in touch with metropolitan society.

Castle Campbell, in Clackmannanshire, painted by Hugh W. Williams, in 1803.

Swiss Cottage, in Cahir, County Tipperary, c. 1820.

An engraved-glass window from Swiss Cottage.

Swiss Cottage is worth comparing with the "cabin" built for or by Jean-Jacques Rousseau near the chateau of Ermenonville, where he spent the last years of his life. The cabin, as described in an anonymous *Tour to Ermenonville* (1785), was "built against the rock and thatched with heath. Within, besides a plain and unornamented fireplace, we found a seat cut out of the rock, and covered with moss, a small table and two wicker chairs." On the door was the inscription "It is on the tops of mountains that man contemplates the face of nature with real delight. There it is that, in conference with the fruitful parent of all things, he receives from her those all powerful inspirations, which lift the mind above the sphere of error and prejudice."

The cabin clearly related to rustic hermitages in English gentlemen's parks, but it related with a difference. For one thing it was not in a park; it was on a hilltop in what contemporaries called a "desert," a stretch of completely unimproved heath a mile or two from the chateau. Round the chateau itself its owner had created conventionally picturesque grounds in the English manner, complete with an artificial cascade and a monument to Rousseau, erected after his death on an island in a lake. The English visitor was struck by the contrast between all this and the adjacent "desert." Rousseau himself had used the cabin on "excursions, during which he loved to read the great book of nature, on the tops of mountains, or in the depths of some venerable forest."

A new note is being struck, the note of the Romantic Movement, which grew out of appreciation of the picturesque, overlapped it, but was essentially different from it. Wild natural scenery ceased to be looked at with a critical eye, as something to be enjoyed but also improved, in the light of a literary or artistic tradition; the simple life ceased to be seen as a form of agreeable play-acting. Nature, in the sense of actual wild landscape not a lost ideal, was now to be approached with reverence, as a means of regeneration and a source of mystical experience. Rousseau was a pioneer, but in the first half of the nineteenth century the attitudes he had helped to inaugurate spread through the Western world.

The idea of the picturesque had inevitably come to America, but its American devotees were at a disadvantage. America had no ruined abbeys, castles, or temples, nor landscapes rich with suitable associations. For a time Americans felt deprived when they looked at their own scenery. The Romantic Movement reversed the situation. "All nature is here new to art," English-born Thomas Cole wrote of the Catskill Mountains in the 1830s, in celebration not in a mood of despondency. "No Tivolis, Ternis, Mont Blancs, Plinlimmons, hackneyed and worn by the pencils of hundreds, but primeval forests, virgin lakes and waterfalls." (Quoted by Charles Rockwell, *The Catskill Mountains*, 1873.) "Here,"

Catskill Mountain House, painted by Thomas Cole, 1830s.

19

wrote American-born Washington Irving in *Home Authors and Home Artists,* "are locked up mighty forests which have never been invaded by the axe; deep umbrageous valleys where the virgin soil has never been outraged by the plough; bright streams flowing in untasked idleness, unburthened by commerce, unchecked by the mill. This mountain zone is in fact the great poetical zone of our country."

As early as 1823–24 the hotel known as the Catskill Mountain House was built on the edge of a cliff in the heart of the range. Forty years later it was still going strong, and being celebrated in verse by Charles Rockwell:

> *There it stands, to bless the pilgrim*
> *From the city's heated homes.*
> *Worn and weary with life's contest*
> *To this mountain height he comes.*

By the middle decades of the century spreading railways and growing cities were bringing more and more visitors to mountainous or wild country all over America. Its apparently inexhaustible wealth of wild landscape was accepted as one of its chief glories; so was the role of this landscape as a source of cleansing, refreshment, and spiritual recharging for tired city-dwellers.

The summer rush to the wilds brought architectural problems. A tent and a campfire may have been the ideal equipment with which to commune with nature, but more permanent forms of settlement inevitably developed, even if they continued to be called "camps." What were these to look like, and how could they best be fitted into wild surroundings? Any idea that wild nature could or should be "improved" had been jettisoned, nor was there any desire to interpose a barrier of cultivation between dwelling and surroundings. The Catskill Mountain House seemed to have been dropped on the edge of its precipice in an almost unaltered landscape. But the hotel itself was a porticoed neoclass-

Leyswood, a house in Sussex by Richard Norman Shaw, 1868–69.

Kragsyde, a house at Manchester-by-the-Sea, by Peabody and Stearns, c. 1882.

Living room of the manor house at Camp Uncas in the Adirondacks. photographed by R. T. Stratton, 1896.

ical building, such as could have been found on the edge of dozens of American cities. Thomas Cole, in his superb picture of hotel and mountains, had to paint the hotel narrow-end on, in order to keep it from being too obtrusive.

For a time experiments were made with the Swiss-chalet style, as on occasions in England. Later on in the century Norman Shaw's houses exerted a powerful influence on American seaside and holiday architecture, mainly on the strength of the brilliant drawings with which they had been illustrated in English architectural magazines. The rocky settings of Cragside and Leyswood were not all that different from the rocky coastline of New England; both Shaw's architecture and the style of draftsmanship with which it was presented are immediately recognizable in Eldon Deane's drawings of summer cottages at Manchester-by-the-Sea. One of them was even called Kragsyde.

But in these and other summer cottages up and down the coast Shaw's architecture was already undergoing a process of simplification, designed to make it more "natural." Boulders were incorporated into foundations as well as left littered over the surrounding ground. Detail was eliminated and the houses covered with a skin of shingles that rapidly weathered to a color in harmony with their setting. Inside, Shaw's great inglenook fireplaces were simplified until they became caves of rough-hewn stone. An extra repertory of forms was drawn from America's brand of natural architecture, the log cabin. It was a form of construction that both made sense in practical terms and had the right connotations; it became especially popular for camps in the Adirondacks, and other mountain districts.

By the early 1900s there were local and individual variations, but a brotherhood of plan, materials, motifs, and descriptive language united holiday houses and camps in wild country all over North America. "The outside will weather to nature's gray, which, combined with the natural effect of the porch and the rough stonework will cause the building to blend into the landscape." The description (from W. T. Comstock's *Bungalows, Camps and Mountain Houses*, 1908) is of a holiday house on the St. Lawrence River, but similar descriptions were being applied to Adirondack camps, or weekend cottages on Signal Mountain in Tennessee. Boulders or rough-hewn stonework were *de rigueur* for fireplaces as well as foundations and chimneystacks, especially for the great stone fireplace that invariably dominated the living room. Walls were normally of timber, either shingle-clad or of exposed logs, carrying the mark of the adze or sometimes with the bark left on them.

Occasionally *cottage-ornée* techniques were revived, and porches, verandahs, and even furniture were made of untrimmed roots, trunks, and branches. The oddest example of this was the New Inn in Estes Park, Colorado, built c. 1906–

10 by Enos A. Mills, naturalist and pioneer of National Parks. Every conceivable detail, inside and out, was made from the bleached and twisted remains of an adjacent stretch of fire-killed forest. It looked (according to *Sunset: The Pacific Monthly*, May, 1921) as though "it had been shaped by the same slow acting elemental forces that had shaped the region." The main bedroom in Kamp Kill Kare in the Adirondacks is almost equally strange: the bed incorporates an entire tree, with a stuffed owl perched on its branches, and the fireplace looks like a mountain cairn with a hole in it. Such features were occasional eccentricities, but other furnishings suited to the simple life became commonplace: rocking chairs, built-in benches, simply patterned hangings, bed-covers and cushions made from Indian or other native textiles, native pottery, and huge iron cooking pots and traditional kitchen cranes, to embellish the living-room fireplace.

The planning and disposition of the houses had to live up to two sets of standards. They had to cater to a life ostensibly "dominated by nature and its ways." Easy access to water, for boating, fishing, or swimming, was almost invariable, and so was a verandah set with rocking chairs and overlooking water or forest; in the William A. Read camp in the Adirondacks there were two, one cantilevered out into the treetops, one over the water. Uncovered balconies were a popular feature, on which to savor the "perfect joy of a night under the canopy of stars." (*Craftsman*, May, 1911) But houses were also expected to cause the minimum disturbance to their setting, to be "of the woods woodsy, seeming a part of their natural surroundings." (*Country Life*, December, 1923) Contemporary descriptions mention with approval efforts to "leave the grounds in the natural rough state" and to cut down the minimum of trees in order to fit in the requisite accommodation. This attitude was often symbolized by a tree left standing within inches of a wall or window, or even growing through a verandah. In order to minimize their impact, camps were often broken up into a number of smaller units, sometimes joined to each other by a covered way. Tact was necessary because the bigger camps could include accommodation for sixty or seventy guests, along with a complex back-up of servants and services. The Vanderbilts, Morgans, and Huntingtons who holidayed in the Adirondacks did not want the simple life to be too simple. A description of an evening at Kamp Kill Kare in the winter of 1899 captures the atmosphere. "Inside the bright fires blazed from great stone fireplaces, and the table was spread with all the delicacies one would expect to find at Delmonico's." (Craig Gilborn, *Durant; The Fortunes and Woodland Camps of a Family in the Adirondacks*, 1981.)

The conventions of camp and cottage life had been set by 1910, and changed remarkably little in the 1920s. They were still going strong in the 1930s, when Frank Lloyd

21

TOP: Bedroom at Kamp Kill Kare in the Adirondacks, photographed by Richard J. Linke, 1974.
ABOVE: Verandah of the Adirondack lodge of William A. Read, photographed in 1907 for House & Garden.

The Read camp in 1982, photographed by Harvey H. Kaiser.

Wright designed Fallingwater. To a considerable extent he and the Kaufmanns worked within them. Fallingwater incorporates open terraces that could be used for sleeping out, and covered ones from which to enjoy woods and water exposed to fresh air but sheltered from sun. Chimneystacks and fireplaces are of rough stonework; the *in situ* boulder that projects as a hearth through the living-room floor could be seen as Wright's development of the traditional boulder fireplace. There is a cooking pot, a crane, and plenty of Indian fabrics and pottery. Existing trees were disturbed as little as possible, and a beam was cast with a kink in order to leave a large one growing untouched in front of the entrance. There is no garden by Fallingwater; any new planting was carefully designed to merge into the forest surroundings. Guest accommodation is in a separate building, joined to the main one by a covered way. The use of concrete instead of timber was unusual, but not unique: a fishing lodge built of stone and concrete, in order to be fireproof, was featured in the *Craftsman* of May, 1911. Even the language in which Fallingwater is sometimes described ("it seems part of the rock formations to which it clings," etc.) follows the conventions.

In fact this kind of description is not especially apt; and Fallingwater is on a different creative level from Adirondack camps or the great majority of holiday cottages. However, this is not because it rejects the conventions that lay behind them but because it transforms them, through new technology, the injection of a second tradition, and the working of a creative imagination. The second tradition is, of course, that of China and Japan, where wild landscapes had been appreciated centuries before the Picturesque Movement got under way in Europe. Moreover in China and Japan, unlike Europe, houses were frequently built in natural settings next to waterfalls, as places from which priests or scholars could commune with the spirits that were thought to live in wild places. Such combinations were depicted in Chinese and Japanese prints and drawings that Wright both knew of and owned. They may have influenced the siting of Fallingwater.

But the style in which such landscapes were depicted was probably as important for Wright. In *The Japanese Print: An Interpretation* (1912) he analyzed what he unwillingly called conventionalization: the way in which, in Japanese and other arts, natural forms were transformed through knowledge and love into another medium, without being killed through imitation. It was an approach that can be savored in his own perspective drawing for Fallingwater. It enabled him to get away from the "natural" approach epitomized at its most naive by walls of boulders or bark-encrusted verandahs, and poise a clearly man-made structure in perfect harmony above a waterfall.

Mark Girouard

OPPOSITE: Ono Falls, by Hokusai, formerly in the collection of Frank Lloyd Wright.

FOREWORD

Fallingwater, Known and Unknown

Fallingwater is famous; from all over the world many thousands of visitors come each year to its remote site. What draws them?—a most unusual house in an exceptionally picturesque setting and, something more, a reputation. In 1936, even before it was finished, knowledgeable people talked about this new work of Frank Lloyd Wright. It upset the experts' opinion that the contentious old American architect (he was then nearing seventy) had nothing of value to add to his achievements. In fact, this house and three more individually superlative buildings that went up almost simultaneously announced an entire new quarter-century of Wright's ebullient creativity.

Fallingwater itself was quickly and widely displayed in exhibitions, in magazines and newspapers, and in many books. After a time a consensus arose that Wright had created a masterwork that appealed not only to professionals but to the public generally. Fallingwater was not much like the earlier architecture that had made Wright famous; it was just as distant from the avant-garde styles of the 1930s, and surely unlike any popular "dream house." Yet now that Fallingwater has been tested by half-a-century of the widest exposure, one can say that it marks a high point in Wright's vast *oeuvre*, in American architecture, in the architecture of this century, and possibly in all architecture.

28 *Fallingwater aroused wide interest when* Time *chose Frank Lloyd Wright for its cover of January 17, 1938; the house appeared in the background and was described inside. The January* Architectural Forum *was wholly devoted to Wright, who directed the layouts and presented Fallingwater amply. At this time the house was given a special exhibition at the Museum of Modern Art, New York. By March it was featured in the Sunday Magazine of the* St. Louis Post-Dispatch.

Fallingwater is famous, but decades of commentaries and critiques have not succeeded in making some of its puzzling aspects more understandable. Why, for instance, did Frank Lloyd Wright select a seemingly inadequate site, perhaps even a dangerous one? Was he, as claimed, following a suggestion of the client? If so, why did the client say that he expected to look from his house toward the waterfall rather than dwell above it? Why is the view from the house confined by placing the building low in the glen where Bear Run flows? Why is the front door inconspicuous, and why, once within the building, are the ceilings low? Granted that the architect decided to lift the main room over the stream just where the waterfall breaks, why was the structure freely cantilevered, why not bridged, anchored at both ends? Was reinforced concrete the best material to embody the architectural idea? And why should the stone walls be aggressively rough, as rough inside as out? What, too, of the proliferation of terraces, so that almost as much built area stands roofless around the house as is enclosed within it? What can have persuaded the client to accept this spendthrift scheme? What is the likelihood that Wright chose a particular boulder top as the hearth in the living room (from which all levels of the house were determined) because he thought it was "Kaufmann's favorite spot for lying in the sun and listening to the falls"? Such questions could be multiplied, and to answer them calls for more than common sense and insider's knowledge. It calls for a probing of Wright's architecture. Then answers begin to be surprising.

No doubt the greatest puzzle posed by Fallingwater is more basic than those just listed. It is this: why does a house designed by an architectural individualist for the special purposes of a special client appeal so much to the public in general? And what does it contribute to the art of architecture if its character is so circumscribed? One part of the answer is that Fallingwater is a happy flowering of Frank Lloyd Wright's genius, a great work of art. Yet underneath the effects of great art—however masterly and ingenious—there lies a consistency of the whole. To understand this quality one must consider those principles that guided the artist. In Wright's statements his principles are denoted by words embodying deep intuitions: *organic, democratic, plasticity, continuity.* During careful study of his texts and his architecture, I have come to believe that these terms present different aspects of one central insight. To Wright, architecture was a great inclusive agency through which humankind adapted the environment to human needs and, reciprocally, attuned human life to its cosmos; amid continual changes architecture could keep human life more natural and nature more humane. This idea pervades Fallingwater in accord with the aims of both architect and client, and gives it not only basic meaning but also powerful subliminal appeal. Personal recollections, some facts, and ideas tested by time will help me to illustrate this.

A few old postcards survive to show the falls on Bear Run before the house was built. From 1890 on, various Masonic groups operated the property as a vacation club, as is indicated on this photograph. Then, in 1916 Kaufmann's Department Stores began to use the property as an employees' camp; in 1921 my parents built a small pre-cut cottage there for their own use. By 1933 they bought the property outright; it had become an important part of family life.

RECOLLECTING
FALLINGWATER

Drifting Toward Wright

In 1927 Janssen began to transform the ground floor of the family store; in 1930 it presented the full art deco effect seen here. Janssen influenced the Kaufmanns' tastes so that they became open to the trend of Wright's more profound art.

As a small boy in Pittsburgh I spent hours at the Carnegie Museum, absorbed in the tinted, full-scale plaster casts of architecture; these fragments of monuments from all ages appealed to me more than the other art on view. Fortunately my parents were attracted to the arts. When I was ten they took me along for a year's trip abroad. My favorite buildings then were the Sainte Chapelle, Paris, and San Clemente, Rome, but in Egypt the ancient, ominous ruins repelled me.

A Pittsburgh architect, Benno Janssen, had become a friend of my parents; two of our early homes (both rented) were designed by him. In 1924 he built a suburban home for us; it echoed old country houses in Normandy. One evening at that home, while my parents were upstairs, Frank Lloyd Wright and I were in the living room having cocktails. Wright looked around at the fumed oak beams, the Samuel Yellin ironwork everywhere, the French and Company furniture. "Edgar," he said, smiling, "Something's Wrong." But he didn't say it to his clients.

Long before, Sam Yellin, a delightful soul, had introduced me to Weyhe's bookshop in New York. Thanks to Erhard Weyhe I began to be aware of books on architecture; no one could have been a gentler guide. It was he, I feel sure, who led me to Henry-Russell Hitchcock's early book, *Modern Architecture, Romanticism and Reintegration.* The writing was sometimes too much for me, and I took refuge in the informative illustrations. Hitchcock, nevertheless, opened my eyes wider than more popular writers; all of whom also took Wright into consideration. Certainly it was Weyhe who, later, sold me de Fries's brief book on Wright, with lovely color plates.

In 1926 my father and Janssen began to plan a grand remodeling of the ground floor of the family's department store in downtown Pittsburgh. This was carried out in bold art deco, black glass columns, light-yellow wood counters, built-in illumination, and murals depicting a history of trade painted by Boardman Robinson. Famous for his cartoons in *The Masses*, Robinson was a perfect gentleman-bohemian. Many such came to the suburban house; somehow expatriate Viennese were numerous. Joseph Urban appeared; he created a fairy-tale ballroom for the main hotel in Pittsburgh and a cheerful swimming-pool hall for a Jewish settlement house our family supported. Paul Frankl, a friend of Frank Lloyd Wright, taught me tricks of crayon rendering and decorated a *pied-à-terre* for my mother. In New York I admired works from the Wiener Werkstätte at Rena Rosenthal's shop, and entire interiors by Winold Reiss, Lucian Bernhard, and Eugene Schoen. Vally Wieselthier, a potter and friend of Paul Lester Wiener, a prominent architect, persuaded me, and then my parents, that I should study art in Vienna. I had resisted going

to college, so I enjoyed my year in Vienna, but not the free-wheeling instruction at the Kunstgewerbeschule.

Then, fortunately, I was able to study in Florence with Victor Hammer, a portraitist and craftsman my mother had lately met in London; it happened he too was Viennese. As one of his apprentices I learned to draw what I saw and to help in the hand-printing workshop. I progressed from admiring San Clemente to being gripped by Brunelleschi's immense vision in Santo Spirito—architecture began to take on a deeper reality at that point. Hammer recommended the books of Gottfried Semper, the nineteenth-century architectural theorist now widely recognized but then still forgotten. Semper had strongly influenced John Wellborn Root in Chicago and Otto Wagner in Vienna, two architects Wright especially admired. My years in Florence were truly educational, but the rigors of the Great Depression pulled me back to the United States.

36

How Fallingwater Began

Settled in New York, a would-be painter of twenty-four, I felt disconnected from the thoughts and ways of America after long study in Europe. A friend recommended Frank Lloyd Wright's *An Autobiography*; reading it I believed Wright saw what I was missing. I went out to Spring Green in Wisconsin, and Wright agreed to let me join the Taliesin Fellowship in October, 1934, though I had no plan to become an architect. Soon my parents came to visit; they were moved by the extraordinary beauty of Wright's home and its landscape, and impressed by the devoted enthusiasm of the apprentices. Wright and my father were both outgoing, winning, venturesome men, and father quickly felt the power of Wright's genius. Mrs. Wright and my mother were cosmopolitan, and romantic in their taste for poetry; mother responded to Mrs. Wright's courageous character. Before the year's end Wright stopped off in Pittsburgh to discuss several projects with my parents; one was a country house to replace a rudimentary cottage that had served for over a decade. Father and Wright drove to the mountain property to consider a site; I went along. This was Wright's first view of our forested land and its waterfall. Sun, rain, and hail accented the rugged terrain and the swollen stream. Wright was led down old stone steps to a flat expanse of rock at the base of the falls; here we and our friends liked to bask between forays into the ever-icy water. Looking up Wright must have been fascinated by the torrent pouring over the fractured ledge; he saw a great opportunity for architecture.

Bear Run flows beneath rugged ledges and over smooth rock shaped by glaciers, constantly changing its song.

OPPOSITE: Another postcard from the days of the Shriners. The double-decked terrain was unified when Wright built the house above the falls.

The frontispiece to the January, 1938, issue of Architectural Forum *was this photograph of Wright. The two apprentices at the extreme right were most concerned with the construction of Fallingwater—Bob Mosher and Edgar Tafel.*

Wright's farseeing area plan, Broadacre City, in a model built by the apprentices in the winter of 1934–35. It was trucked to New York for exhibition in Rockefeller Center.

At Taliesin, I, too, was enthusiastic; indeed, waking up in that marvelous place still seems one of my most profound experiences. Happily, the Fellowship was preparing a large model demonstrating Wright's plan for a new and better community, Broadacre City he called it. This permitted me to learn about his sense of architecture as the matrix of human relationships. Without aiming to practice architecture I could benefit from his encompassing view of the art. Every day at teatime Wright would talk informally to the apprentices, often about ideas stimulated by Broadacre. On Sunday at breakfast he would speak more deliberately on general themes. Wright believed that if arts were to bloom and be fruitful they must be well-rooted in the soil of everyday life. I was particularly impressed by Wright's explaining his own work and then, before long, presenting paradoxical interpretations. It was his way of weaning apprentices from dependence on ready-made solutions; he forced us to reconsider whatever certainties we might have uncritically adopted. There were hard edges to his teaching balanced by exceptional charm and humor, and quick

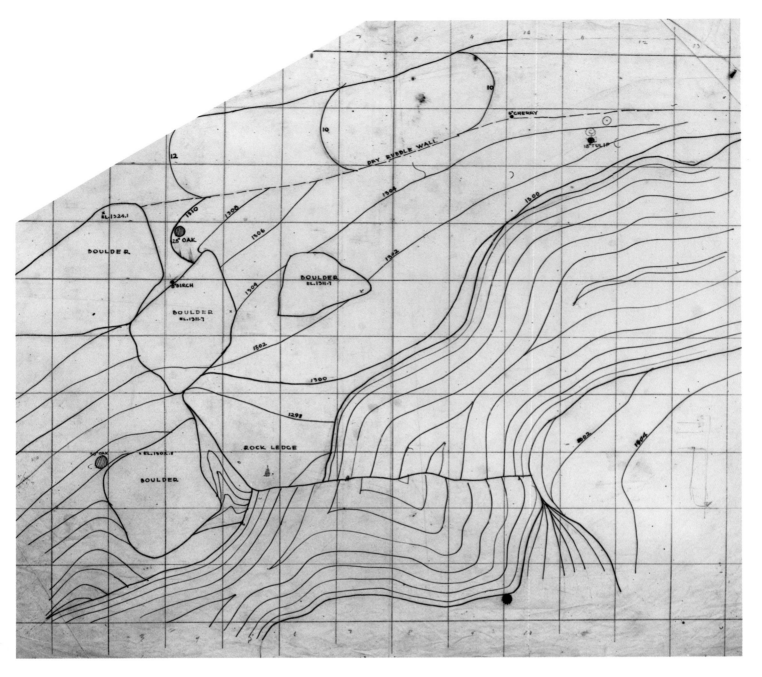

The labels visible on the contour map include: BOULDER, 25" OAK, BIRCH, BOULDER EL.1311-7, ROCK LEDGE, DRY RUBBLE WALL, CHERRY, 18" TULIP, EL.1324.1, and various elevation contour numbers (1310, 1308, 1306, 1304, 1302, 1300, 1298).

A contour map of terrain around the Bear Run falls was rescaled for use in Wright's drafting room as shown here.

sympathy for the efforts of those less experienced. So strong and convincing were Wright's principles that after a while—since I was not attuned to the Fellowship routine—it was time for me to leave, indelibly influenced by Wright. By then being a painter had lost its significance for me, and I went to work at the family department store.

In September, 1935, when on business in the Middle West, father arranged to drive to Taliesin to find out what Wright had in mind for the country house. The intervening months had produced correspondence but no drawings. Wright had received a contour map of the area dominated by the falls, with large boulders and trees indicated; he was mulling over his ideas. Just before father arrived Wright made the first sketches of the concept of Fallingwater, and initial plans and elevations were prepared. Selecting a tall boulder as the anchor of his design, Wright swung the main spaces outward: to the east the entrance, to the south the big room extending over the falls, to the west the kitchen, and to the north stairs and hallways.

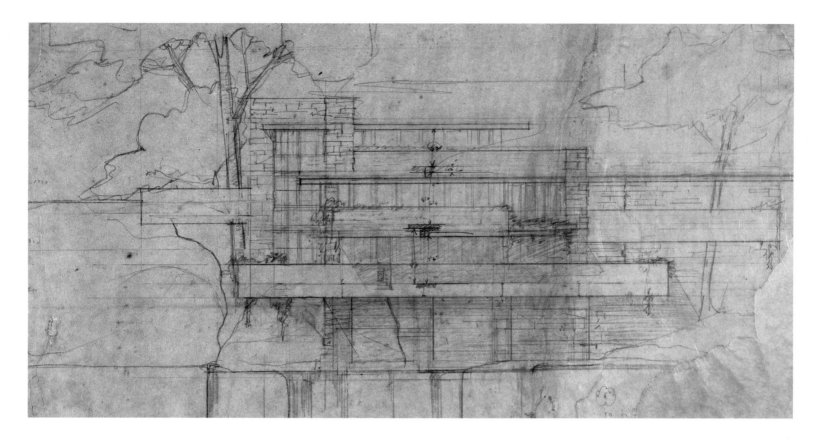

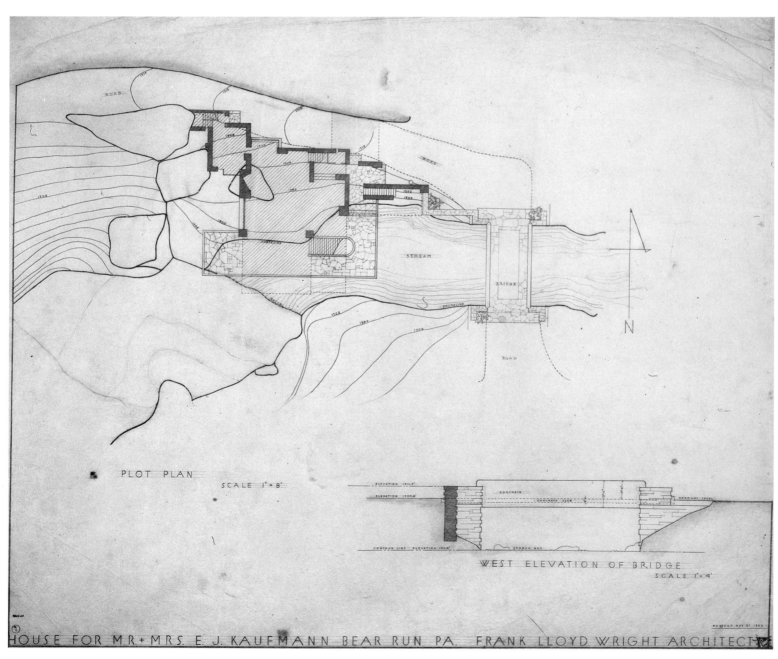

PLOT PLAN

SCALE 1'= 8'

WEST ELEVATION OF BRIDGE

SCALE 1'= 4'

HOUSE FOR MR.+ MRS. E.J. KAUFMANN BEAR RUN PA. FRANK LLOYD WRIGHT ARCHITECT

A month later a full set of drawings reached Pittsburgh; my father, my mother, and I sat down to examine them. The main house was drawn up, but an addition for guests, servants, and garage was intended (and in 1939 completed). It was an extraordinary moment when the full force of Wright's concept became apparent. We did not hesitate; whatever the previous expectations and whatever the problems suggested by the plans, here was an amazing augmentation of our regular refreshment in nature, and a magnetic image. The prospects were exhilarating. Father enjoyed bold ideas and challenges, especially in design and construction. My mother found sources of graceful livability in an unusual setting. I was eager to witness the actualization of Wright's designs.

Wright and father informally agreed on a division of responsibilities for the construction. Wright selected a contractor to oversee concrete and stone work. It was a risky choice, for Wright had never seen the man. Apprentices from Taliesin were sent, one after another, to represent the architect. (One, Edgar Tafel, has published his reminiscences; the others were

OPPOSITE, ABOVE: The earliest surviving elevation of Fallingwater shows the house practically as built.
OPPOSITE, BELOW: An early floor plan of the house locates it precisely in the irregular terrain.

BELOW: A basement plan of Fallingwater indicates how the house is fitted in among boulders. The top of the boulder on the right serves as the hearth in the living room. The two small rooms now contain the heating plant (right) and general storage (left).

41

OVERLEAF: A perspective view of Fallingwater, largely drawn by Wright. He used it as background to his portrait on the cover of Time. *Later drawings show rounded edges on slabs and horizontal parapets, but this is almost the only change introduced.*

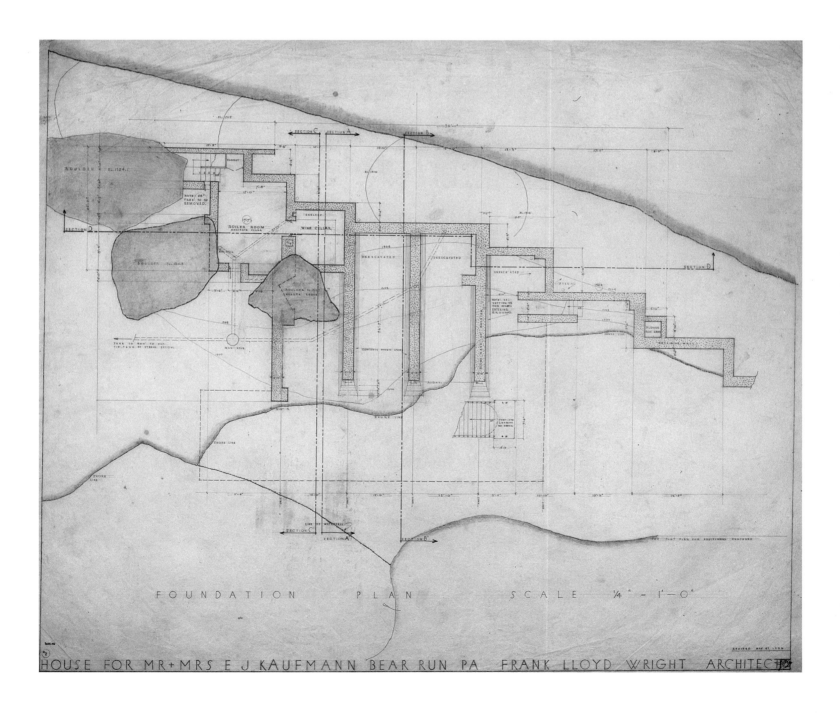

FOUNDATION PLAN   SCALE ¼" = 1'-0"

HOUSE FOR MR + MRS E J KAUFMANN BEAR RUN PA   FRANK LLOYD WRIGHT ARCHITECT

Stone for walls and floors at Fallingwater was quarried on the property; the photograph above shows the old quarry put to new use in 1935. The center picture gives some idea of the work in progress.

interviewed by Donald Hoffmann for his 1978 book on Fallingwater.) The labor force consisted of local hands who needed to be trained in Wright's individual ways. The bridge over the run was selected as a first effort; it turned out to be far from satisfactory and had to be pulled down. The second try was better, the men were getting into the swing of the job. Consequently, the best stonework in the house is found in the guest wing, the last portion of the house to be built. Utilities—heat-

Workmen adapted to Wright's own way of laying stone; their skill shows especially well here, where walls wrap around the kitchen space and that of the steps down to the basement.

ing, plumbing, and wiring—were installed by city technicians under the guidance of the man responsible for such work in the store and warehouses in town. In this way father hoped to keep down the costs of construction. The program seems to have backfired, and in fact the cost of the total building ran to $145,000—who can estimate the sums spent over the years on correcting the shortcomings of the initial construction?

It was two years after the first drawings had reached us

MR.EDGAR J.KAUFMANN(KAUFMANN'S FIFTH AVENUE:
PITTSBURGH,PENNA.

Says you can get
and there

My dear E.J.:   If you are paying to have the
concrete engineering done down there there is
no use whatever in our doing it here. I am willing
you should take it over but I am not willing to
be insulted.

So we will send no more steel diagrams. I am unaccustomed to such treatment where I have built
buildings before and do not intend to put up with
it now so I am calling Bob back until we can work
out something or nothing.

Also it appears that an attitude has developed on
your part - "what does the architect know about what
I want - I am going to live in this house - not he".
Now I have heard that provincialism from women but
never before from a man. And it isn't too late yet for
you to get an architect that does know what you want.

I don't know what kind of architect you are familiar
with but it apparantly isn't the kind I think I am.
You seem not to know how to treat a decent one. I
have put so much more into this house than you or
any other client has a right to expect that if I
haven't your confidence -to hell with the whole thing.

Sincerely yours,

Frank Lloyd Wright, Architect
TALIESIN:SPRING GREEN:WISCONSIN:AUGUST 27th, 1936

46   *Wright's letter and my father's reply; the former is*
shown by permission of the Frank Lloyd Wright
Foundation. These letters are dated only a day apart,
which is not possible; perhaps the Taliesin letter was
sent a day or two earlier.

that we moved into an incomplete Fallingwater. Meanwhile I
had been acting as an *ad hoc* and inexperienced intermediary
between Frank Lloyd Wright and his agents on the one hand
and my parents and their advisors on the other. There were
innumerable questions of money and adjustments of understanding. In the summer of 1936 it looked as if an impasse had
been reached. Wright felt slighted by interference in the building process. I became embroiled in the realities of architecture
and began to understand some of the qualities of Fallingwater.

The reason that prompted Wright to complain soon came
to light, and although my father was ignorant of it he had, in
fact, induced it. When the main-floor slab was being cast,
concrete beams that extended eighteen feet beyond the stub
supporting walls were given twice the weight of reinforcing
rods that Wright had specified. Pittsburgh engineers advising
my father had redrawn the plans, adding steel, for safety as
they saw it. My father's supervisor on the job approved this,
and Wright's representative accepted it. Thus, without spe-
cific permission by architect or client a hazardous load was
added to the cantilevering. Father had been wrong in allowing
the engineers so much authority. His claim that Wright should
supervise more, in person, was also true, and thereafter
Wright visited the construction at four- or six-week intervals.

Despite this painful experience my father persisted, for a
spell, in suggesting alternatives to Wright's plans. One such
event I described in 1962 as follows:

August 28th, 1936.

Dear Mr. Wright:

If you have been paid to do the concrete engineering up there there is no use whatever of our doing it down here. I am not willing to take it over as you suggest nor am I willing to be insulted.

So if you will not send any more steel diagrams, what shall I do? I am unaccustomed to such treatment where I have been building before and I do not intend to put up with it now so I am calling upon you to come down here, which I hoped you could have done during the past few weeks, to inspect the work under Mr. Hall's direction who is an unknown foreman to you, instead of allowing the entire responsibility of his craftsmanship to rest upon us here. So if you will come here perhaps we can work out something or nothing.

, Also it appears that an attitude has developed on your part - what does the client know about what he wants - I am building the house not he and he will have to live according to how I plan it. Now it is true that here we live in a province and that provincialism from both men and women exists, and it is for that reason that I put my confidence and hope in an architect who was not barb-wired by such provincialism. There are certain elements in our living at Bear Run that are so much a part of our lives, such as water and outdoor sleeping, that I feel the plans to date are still leaving us in the dark as to how they are to be accomplished.

I don't know what kind of clients you are familiar with but apparently they are not the kind I think I am. You seem not to know how to treat a decent one. I have put so much

confidence and enthusiasm behind this whole project in my limited way, to help the fulfillment of your efforts that if I do not have your confidence in the matter - to hell with the whole thing.

Sincerely yours,

[signature: Edgar J. Kaufmann]

Mr. Frank Lloyd Wright,
Taliesin,
Spring Green, Wisconsin.

P.S. Now don't you think that we should stop writing letters and that you owe it to the situation to come to Pittsburgh and clear it up by getting the facts? Certainly there are reasons which must have prompted you to write as you have.

I am sorry that you are calling Bob back. He seems entirely wrapped up in his work and in its progress but this is beyond my control and you must use your own judgment.

It is difficult for me to conceive that a man of your magnitude and understanding could write such a letter. In deference to our past association I must naturally put it aside as if it had never been written as it certainly does not conform to the facts.

The most westerly extension of the house is an open terrace cantilevered far into space. It is supported by a large reinforced concrete beam on its long axis, and by several transverse ones. The main beam is anchored in the great chimney mass; the lesser ones in a natural boulder nearby. Under the main beam, well back out of sight, a stone supporting wall ran for a number of feet. Here the Pittsburgh engineers were certain of their ground; this was a structure they knew how to calculate, for it was practically independent of the complicated stresses of the main house. They knew that, as it was, the terrace must fall; they knew that just four more feet of that inconspicuous base wall would avoid the disaster. My father called Wright's young apprentice, and ordered the four feet built. Wright himself came around in due course of inspection and said nothing. Another month passed and Wright came again, went over the work with father, and no word of the wall. At the day's end, over a comfortable drink in the half-finished shell of the house, father confessed to Wright and said "If you've not noticed it in these last two tours of inspection, there can't be anything very bad about it, architecturally." "E. J.," said Wright, "come with me." They went out to the spot in question and, behold, the top four inches of the additional wall were gone! "When I was here last month," Wright continued, "I ordered

the top layers of stone removed. Now, the terrace has shown no sign of failing. Shall we take down the extra four feet of wall?"

Later, many of father's suggestions were as unsuitable as Wright's idea of gold-leafing the concrete. Yet, in the long run, despite such vagaries these two productive and responsible men enabled a grand architectural concept to take coherent shape.

The Faults of Fallingwater

Mistakes have plagued Fallingwater, yet the extraordinary beauty of the house and the delight it brought to the life of its inhabitants form the context in which its construction should be evaluated. Life at Fallingwater did include flaws and the efforts to overcome them. Before the family moved in, there were doubts about the structure, aroused by written reports from the engineers my father employed to check Wright's working drawings. The building would break apart and fall into the run these reports implied. When father submitted them to Wright there was an outraged response, and father had the good sense to believe his architect. Eventually he interred the reports behind a stone in one of the walls. But uncertainty had been aroused, and when cracks appeared in the east and west parapets of the terrace of the main bedroom it was necessary for Wright to reassure his client that the building was settling, not fracturing. Did they discuss what seems obvious today, fifty years later? Overloading the beams of the main floor with extra heavy reinforcing rods caused the slab to sag more than should have been expected, and since the two floors were tied together—especially by T irons in the window framing of the south front—the upper terrace was bound to follow. Moreover, this upper floor, extending six feet farther than the living room, had been stacked with heavy bags of cement during construction despite objections from Wright's representative. There is no proof that this extra load augmented the damage, yet it was foolhardy. Further cracks developed but the first two were the worst; they kept worrying my father throughout his life. They may have been a burden to the architect as well, if a report is accurate that shortly after construction Wright, in a high fever from pneumonia, was heard to mutter "too heavy." Evidently he was envisaging Fallingwater. Those two cracks require cosmetic patching even today, but there is no evidence of structural failure.

Structural failure is mistakenly deduced from the way horizontal edges of the house dip downward. This is due to

OPPOSITE AND ABOVE: Fallingwater within its scaffolding while the poured concrete cures. The photographs show how rough-and-ready the work really was, and how the contractor's shack was perched at the very edge of the cantilevering.

Another view of the house under construction.

This remarkable view reveals the structure of the horizontal slabs of reinforced concrete, with thin walls ready to carry finished flooring. A thicker (and curved) reinforced-concrete beam is part of the main structural system not made evident in the closed-in house. Below the trellis, which is still cross-braced, the curved hatch awaits the stairway down to the brook.

an oversight in setting up wood forms into which the concrete was poured; they were built level, not sloped upward to allow for settlement when the forms were removed. It is hard to understand how this came about. Wright had considerable familiarity with reinforced concrete, and he was assisted by experienced structural engineers. My father had his own advisers, engineers, and job supervisor. None of these men warned the contractor, who proceeded in sheer ignorance. Considering the various facts it is not surprising that the contractor was frightened to strike out the supports of the forms when the time came. But at Wright's command the posts were struck, and no disaster followed. Much later two subordinate overhangs did fail: the roof over the eastern terrace because of incorrectly placed reinforcing rods, and the trellis over the southerly corner of the living room because a heavy tree branch fell on it during a storm. Both have been satisfactorily rebuilt.

Why do those two major parapet cracks reappear? The answer leads to wider issues. Over the years my father had his engineers reporting on deflections of the concrete; after a while it became obvious that the cantilevers fell and rose in response to temperature changes affecting the materials. Deflection was small in either direction, but the constant movement reopened cracks and strained flashing between roofs and walls, a delicate joint in any building. When the flashing opened up, even inconspicuously, water penetrated, then threaded through interstices, and issued far from the point of entry as distressing leaks. There were seventeen such areas when we first moved in. Roofing and terrace flooring were lifted, stray chunks of sodden lumber were extracted, and sopping sheets of insulation were replaced with dry ones; the house became presentable inside. Had the insulation been wet before it was sealed in? Not unlikely, but damaged flashing was more surely responsible. Some leakage still occurs, and now a concerted effort is under way to rework all flashing. To do this and yet maintain the neatness of the exterior will be a challenge.

Besides these troubles there has always been a question about the parapets: do they strengthen the great horizontal concrete slabs or merely weigh on them? Wright himself after much deliberation believed they helped to carry the load, but not so effectively as he had hoped. It seems to me that, amid a diversity of opinions, this is decisive. The reinforcing rods that run continuously from flat plane into upright parapet help to support and unify the structure.

Do these faults impugn Wright's ability? Comparable situations indicate an answer, bearing in mind that the architect and his client knew the design of Fallingwater was an exploration beyond the limits of conventional practice. The small deflections (up and down) at Fallingwater were not foreseen; neither were those (from side to side) in early skyscrapers, yet these are now accepted as normal. Some of the great monuments of architecture have suffered structural troubles, precisely because they were striving beyond normal limitations. The dome of Hagia Sophia in Constantinople, the belfries of St. Peter's in Rome, the core of the Panthéon in Paris, all

51

BELOW AND OVERLEAF: The isometric perspective drawings presented below and on the next spread show graphically how Wright used concrete and stone in the structure of Fallingwater— level by level, as the house was built.

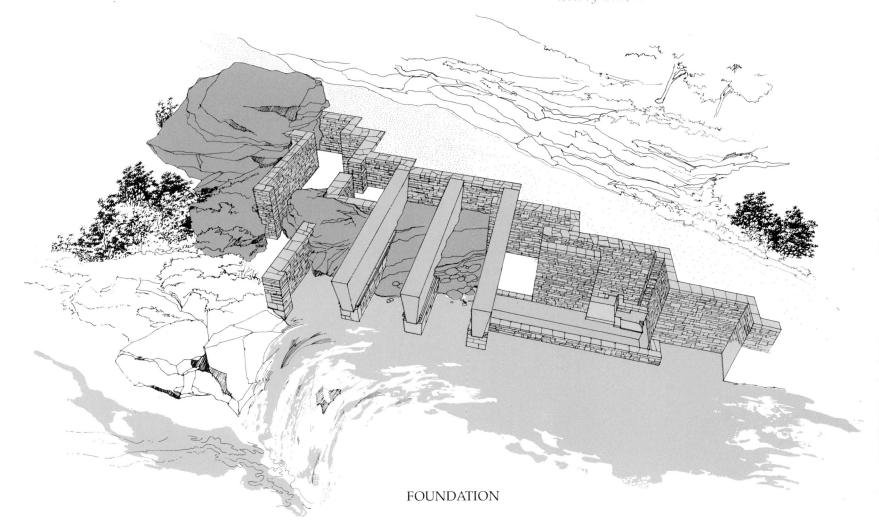

FOUNDATION

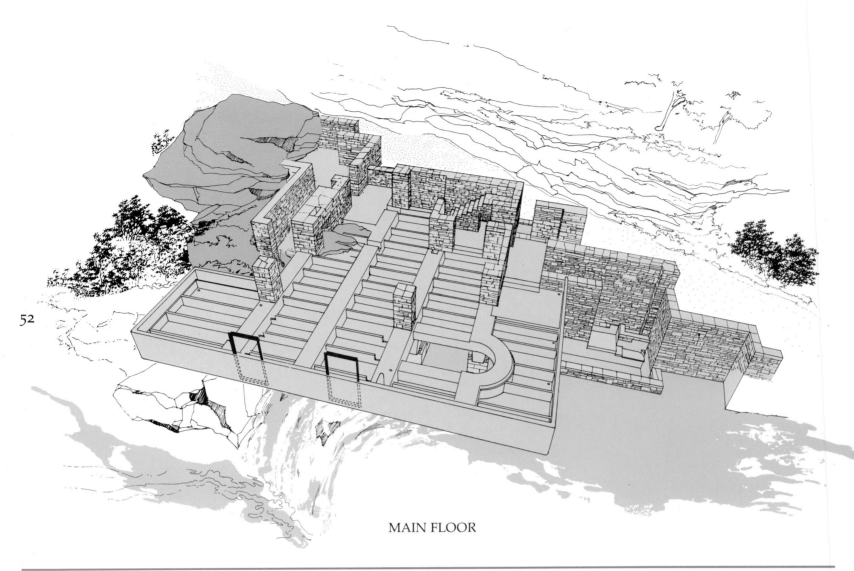

MAIN FLOOR

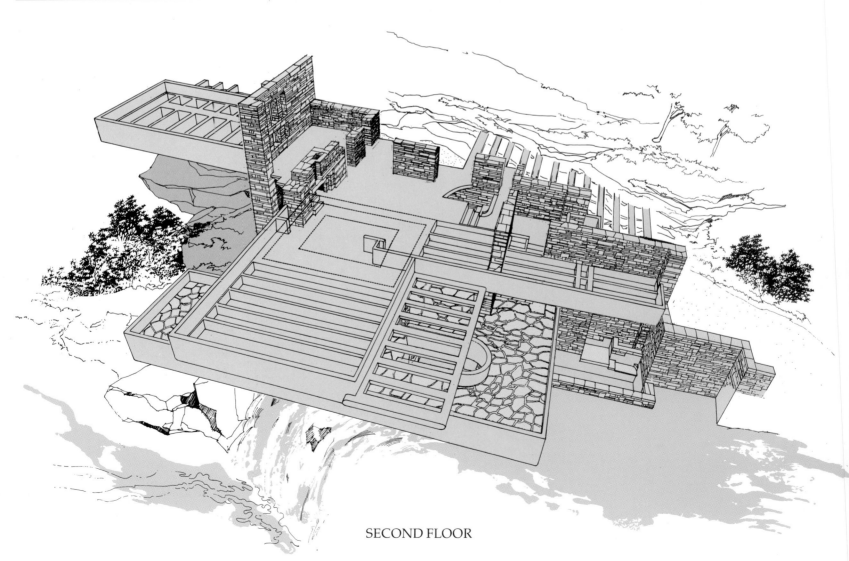

SECOND FLOOR

52

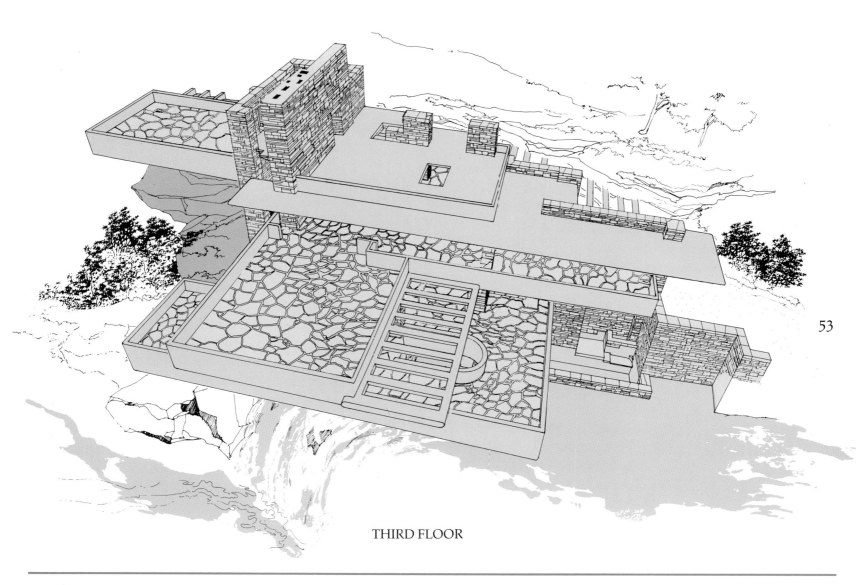

THIRD FLOOR

53

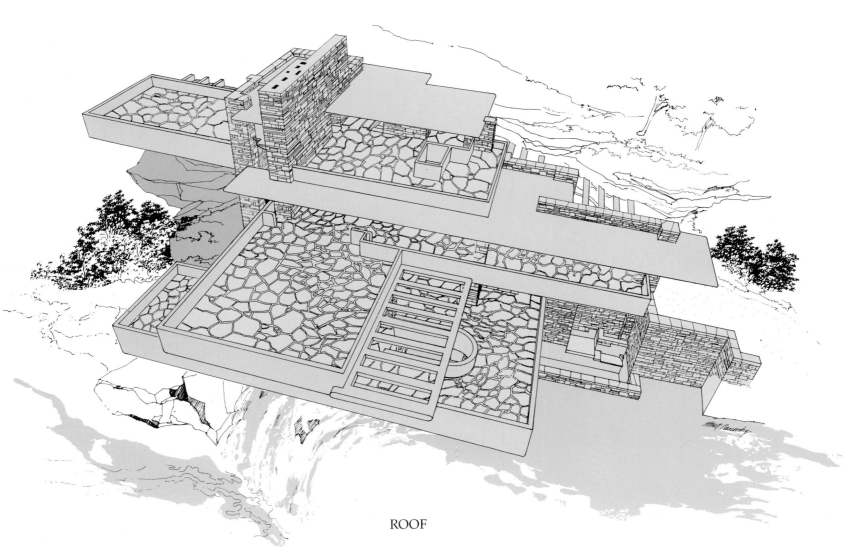

ROOF

threatened the stability of their structures and required drastic repairs, yet these buildings still stand and add glory to their countries and their art. My father was no monarch and his home was not conceived as a public monument, but Wright's genius justifies these references. No apologies are necessary for what he achieved at Fallingwater.

54 *My father inspecting the construction of his house.* *BELOW: The author with a guest on the east terrace.*

OPPOSITE, ABOVE: Albert Einstein and Morris Raphael Cohen attended a conference at Fallingwater, c. 1938. *OPPOSITE, BELOW: My parents on the terrace of the main bedroom:, 1940s.*

Living with Fallingwater

Fallingwater was one of those works by Wright that transformed the world's opinion of his art. From seeming a figure of earlier decades he leapt into view as a bold innovator. Increasing recognition flowed his way, and Fallingwater received its share. One portion of it changed my life: John McAndrew of the Museum of Modern Art in New York mounted a one-building exhibition of the house; not long after, I was asked to join the staff there. I moved from Pittsburgh; however, weekends were usually spent at Fallingwater. This was not difficult, for the journey from New York was convenient then. One boarded a sleeping car at the old Pennsylvania Station and after a comfortable night alit at Greensburg, from where it was a forty-minute drive to the house.

Fallingwater, enmeshed in established habits, soon became part of the family's weekend experience. The beauty that resulted cannot be verbalized any more than the elation this beauty elicited; life simply was raised to a new level. When people ask about this there often seems to be an implicit expectation: great architecture, changing the way people live, must change people. Art may arouse dormant sensibilities, and Fallingwater changed us in this way, I believe. Furthermore, it brought new, usually enjoyable associations.

Occasionally large groups were entertained at Fallingwater, and then cottages surviving from earlier days would be pressed into use for guests who could not be housed in the Wright building. More than ten bodies meant buffet meals on the living room terraces or inside; formality was never considered. One early Christmas season we welcomed a ten-day continual flow of visitors. The logistics must have been formidable, but my parents and the augmented help remained in the best of humors. Guests were either on the staff of the Museum of Modern Art—their interest aroused by the exhibition there—or else close to the Museum, particularly through the grand survey of the Bauhaus it presented. John McAndrew acted as our master of revels. Marcel Breuer, the Moholy-Nagys, the Alfred Barrs, and others drifted in, were merry, and departed in deep snow. About half an hour after the Moholys drove off, the butler came in to announce, "Mr. Mahogany is stuck in a ditch!"

Utterly different was a later gathering invited by my father who, with some associates, hoped to unite different sectors of American Jewry in dealings with the Federal government. Thus high-level advisers to the New Deal and prominent movers among the Jews met for free-ranging discussions, that, alas, produced no appreciable results. I listened, and noticed the meaningful silences of Albert Einstein.

On other occasions guests arrived in small groups or singly, among them Walter Gropius, courteous and reserved; Alvar Aalto and his amiable family were more lively. Henry-Russell Hitchcock came when I was not present, and went wading in the run. My mother told me, "He has the most beautiful feet I've ever seen!" Philip Johnson was distracted by the noise of the waterfall; he said it excited his bladder. But

Approaching Fallingwater, late 1930s, before the Lipchitz statue was placed at the edge of the plunge pool.

OPPOSITE, ABOVE: The western side of Fallingwater.
OPPOSITE, BELOW: The trellis of the living room, seen inside and out.

usually weekends were shared quietly with friends—long walks through the woods, cold plunges under the falls, reading, listening to 78 r.p.m. records, and (what now seems sinful) breakfast in bed after a quick dip. The exhilaration of clean air, the musical murmur of the brook, the restful vistas into endless greens were enhanced by the experience of Fallingwater.

In New York, work at the Museum enlarged my awareness of Wright's position in the development of modern architecture. When museum duties were interrupted for three years' service during World War II, the renown of Fallingwater opened doors in my Australian leave area.

Returning to civilian life I was confronted with changes. Father's health had deteriorated; he had become captious. Mother was weighed down by this and other troubles. Fallingwater had suffered. Closed for lack of fuel it had been racked by raw heat and cold; without ventilation dampness had settled in; and the heavy smoke of wartime freight trains, penetrating the forest, had smudged the exterior. We were eager to get Fallingwater into shape again, but unluckily a latex-based paint, supposedly an improvement, was applied to the concrete; a chilly sheen now separated the building from its surroundings.

My parents had been spending winters in the southern California desert, which they found invigorating; they planned to build a house there by Richard Neutra. This fitted nicely into father's long record of bold building enterprises, and my mother was happy to see him absorbed in a new one. It fell to me to talk of the way this would appear in relation to Fallingwater. The Neutra house would be interpreted as a rejection of Wright, and Wright would be the first person to react. My father agreed to withhold his name from publication of the new house, and during Wright's lifetime it was known merely as "a house in the Arizona desert," as the local area, curiously, was called.

For another half-dozen years I saw father commission a series of designs from Frank Lloyd Wright. As Fallingwater claimed more of the family's activities and affections, we felt some inadequacies of the planning. The entrance could become crowded, and the kitchen, adequate for cooking, provided no space where staff could relax—going back to their rooms was inconvenient. Adjoining the kitchen there was space outdoors under the west terrace where an addition could be built inconspicuously. Father wanted to build it without consulting Wright, and I had to stage a strong protest. Wright designed a very neat and satisfactory adjunct. There were other plans for changes and additions to Fallingwater, none essential and none executed, nor were any of the grandiose projects for Pittsburgh Wright designed for father. This was perhaps inevitable since father was steadily growing more self-preoccupied and Wright was eager to construct great designs at the culmination of his long career. Among Wright's late, ambitious projects only a few were connected with my father; Wright, however, felt their friendship was fading.

In 1952, beset by difficulties, my mother died at Fallingwater; this cast a long shadow over the place. My father now needed constant attention, and two years later he remarried. These family matters influenced the fate of Fallingwater. Father and I had talked earnestly about what would become of the house when he died, in view of his plan to remarry and my decision to remain in New York. We agreed that sooner or later Fallingwater and its grounds should become accessible

59

OPPOSITE: Two views of the entry, outside (above) and inside (below). The glass transom is set farther out than the door, in keeping with the angled forms Wright used throughout. The rugs had to be removed when the house was opened to the public, for everyone must step through here.

The staff's sitting alcove off the kitchen, added in 1946. The glass is not divided by horizontal framing; Wright used this detail at Taliesin West, his Arizona home.

60

to the public. We also agreed that a good portion of his estate should be used to establish a foundation on whose board I, assisted by my uncle, would represent the family. With this support a carefully planned program for Fallingwater could be evolved and implemented. What agency might care for the house? I was unsure that the regular cultural, educational, or governmental institutions would or could present Frank Lloyd Wright's concepts fairly. In Wright's designs and in our experience, the forested grounds and the run were as much a part of the architectural statement as was the structure. Father had become interested in a private organization in Pittsburgh, the Western Pennsylvania Conservancy, active in nature conservation; but it was too early to approach them about Fallingwater. Thus father indicated a direction and provided for funding; we both believed a satisfactory solution would be developed. My father died in 1955 in California, a few hours after Wright had come for a friendly visit.

Two projects for the Bear Run property, neither executed. ABOVE: An entry above the main house, at garage level. BELOW: The "Rhododendron Chapel," intended for meditation.

Responsibilities

The responsibility for Fallingwater passed to me. Although I settled in New York I continued to spend weekends on Bear Run and staffed the house and grounds. Fallingwater began to require more fundamental care than hitherto; the strains of wartime and negligence during the original construction (despite everyone's efforts) were taking their toll. The maintenance and grounds crew was headed by a reliable man my own age and his able assistant. The head gardener was an ace, not native to the area, nor were the household help. All these were old acquaintances, so that managing the estate was not the chore it might have been. Some of my parents' regular guests were no longer alive, and I often invited New York friends to keep me company. This good week-

Two interiors, before the house was put in order, 1937. The chairs, bought in Berlin, 1921, had seats that folded out to form low lounges. The rug in the living room is Berber; that in front of the bed is a flokati from Greece.

The stairs from the living room hatchway, with new, stronger end posts.

OPPOSITE: *Three photographs taken just after the 1956 tornado.* ABOVE: *The grounds across the run from the house, with scaffolding for painting.* BELOW: *Heavy debris caught against the stairs below the living room. Sludge on the east terrace of the living room.*

end life balanced unfamiliar obligations I now faced, the relationship with father's second wife and the formation of his charitable foundation in Pittsburgh. Fallingwater occupied a larger portion of my attention than ever before, and I was grateful to have it so.

After so many years it seemed as if Fallingwater itself were an old reliable friend, well established in its setting—yet new emergencies arose. Spring freshets regularly carried assorted detritus down the run. Every now and then the steel hangers of the steps descending from the living room would be bent by the forceful impact of segments of tree trunks or heavy lumber. Now the steel straps no longer could be straightened. When I asked Mr. Wright what to do, he detailed new, stronger end posts, anchored in bedrock, to shield the stairs. Although this meant that the stairs were not freely suspended, as conceived, the alteration was inconspicuous and effective.

The following summer, August, 1956, Bear Run and Fallingwater both were put to an extraordinary test. One weekend afternoon with the usual company in residence, a freak tornado hit our area square on. Violent rain and wind whipped in; the run rose rapidly above its banks—one could see it expanding minute by minute. For exterior painting, the house was girt in wooden scaffolding that was hung from the parapets on three sides, and gusts of wind shook the gross temporary structure to and fro. The house was being racked. It was terrifying; we were trapped in a house subjected to huge strains no one had ever foreseen. Would it hold up? The outdoor staff stood helpless across the torrent from us. We attempted to loosen nails in the scaffolding to let the lumber be carried away—trying to reduce stress on the building—but the wood, swollen with water, kept a tight grip; the effort was useless. Meanwhile, movable furniture in living room and kitchen was piled up off the floor, for water had risen higher than the terrace parapets. Glass doors were closed and for the most part held tight. The main stairs, however, carried a cascade from the hillside behind the house. Ankle-deep in water, we looked over an alien lake obliterating the glen and shoving restlessly against glass doors, while the wind howled and rain poured down in wild sheets. After some hours the violence subsided and it was possible to slosh up to a relatively intact guest wing. The valiant cook offered to prepare a hot meal in the fireplace there, but a drowned snake that lay nestled in it almost defeated her. The next morning we awoke to a house thick with sludge. The banks of Bear Run were ravaged, large areas of native rhododendron were torn out, smaller boulders were swept away, trees were down. A stout wild grape vine, trained across the brook to adorn the living room trellis, was gone. Two bronze statues, set outdoors near the house, had disappeared, Lipchitz's *Mother and Child* and a Marini horse-

man. As soon as possible the house was thoroughly cleansed, the terrain was replaced, and the Lipchitz, a unique cast, was repaired by the artist. The Marini, made of a soft alloy, was not findable though the glen was thoroughly searched. Most important of all, if a building were in danger of collapse that test would have made it evident; Fallingwater came through structurally unscathed.

In 1962 a detailed account of Fallingwater was published thanks to Professor Bruno Zevi, the Italian architect and author. As editor of the journal *L'architettura,* he devoted a whole issue to Fallingwater, marking its twenty-fifth anniversary. I was happy to write about the house, and an old friend, the architect and designer Paul Mayén, who had been taking informal, perceptive photographs of the house over several years, contributed them for illustrations, many in color. The publication thus produced was often reprinted as long as the plates lasted. But the original transparencies were never returned from Italy despite many requests.

The Lipchitz Mother and Child, *placed by Wright at the corner of the plunge pool. Damaged in the 1956 tornado and repaired by the artist, this statue is now securely held by a strong chain inside the base.*

Rewards and Opportunities

Taking care of Fallingwater was a challenge, enjoying it was the reward. Seasons and years rolled on; I continued to rely on the rhythm, peace, and stimulus of weekends on Bear Run. Fallingwater revealed the profundity of Wright's art more and more the longer I lived with it. How easy to take these luxuries of body and spirit for granted, as inalienable privileges. But, what would happen to Fallingwater after my day?

It became clear that I must try to prepare for the next step. Who would care for Fallingwater understandingly? How might its qualities become more available to more people? Could Fallingwater stay vital?—not a relic but a witness for the future. Three resources were at hand: the increasing fame of Fallingwater, the wisdom and abilities of the men father had chosen to work with me on his foundation, and the funds available through the foundation. The board carefully considered several lines of action; eventually the Western Pennsylvania Conservancy appeared as the best potential recipient. My father had contributed to their programs and thought well of them. The money required would be disbursed in the Pittsburgh area, as was right. But would the Conservancy be tempted to take the responsibility of managing a house for public visitation, a new field for them? Luckily the house was embedded in extensive forests and varied mountain terrain, rich in wildflowers and fauna, elements the Conservancy was set up to save—which also were essential to the quality of Fallingwater.

After much discussion obstacles were overcome, and in the fall of 1963 Fallingwater, supported by a generous but prudent endowment, passed into the possession of the Western Pennsylvania Conservancy. For this the efforts of my associates in the foundation were essential. My own feelings at the time are shown in remarks made at the ceremony of transmission:

> These ceremonies mark the establishment of a new agency of our community: The Kaufmann Conservation on Bear Run, given to the public, in care of Western Pennsylvania Conservancy, as a memorial to my parents, Liliane and Edgar Kaufmann.
>
> Why a memorial to Liliane and Edgar Kaufmann? Because these grounds and this house of theirs were given shape by them, and were vitalized by the happiness which they experienced living here, even years before they built the house. This is their place as it stands. If it is suited to a new existence, that is because they shaped it well.
>
> What are these grounds and this house? Acres of rock and acid earth, second-growth trees and icy streams, roughly cast in the Appalachian mold—and something more: a place of vigorous beauty, of self-renewing enchantment, of adventuresome picturesqueness that answers perfectly a romantic need in modern hearts, the need to be natural, to experience nature not as grist for our mills but as the habitat that has formed us.
>
> Designed for this setting, the house was hardly up before its fame circled the earth; it was recognized as one of the clearest successes of the American genius Frank Lloyd Wright.
>
> It takes but an instant to see the character of the

house; yet, after all these years, there are details and relationships in it which I've discovered only recently. Its beauty remains fresh like that of the nature into which it fits. It has served well as a home, yet has always been more than that, a work of art, beyond any ordinary measures of excellence. Itself an ever-flowing source of exhilaration, it is set on the waterfall of Bear Run, spouting nature's endless energy and grace. House and site together form the very image of man's desire to be at one with nature, equal and wedded to nature.

Without drawing on tradition, without relying on precedent, Fallingwater was created by Frank Lloyd Wright as a declaration that in nature man finds his spiritual as well as his physical energies, that a harmonious response to nature yields the poetry and joy that nourish human living.

Such a place cannot be possessed, it is a work by man for man, not by *a* man for *a* man. Over the years since it was built Fallingwater has grown ever more famous and admired, a textbook example of modern architecture at its best. By its very intensity it is a public resource, not a private indulgence.

Finally, why are these acres and this house given as a conservation, in the care of the Western Pennsylvania Conservancy? Because conservation is not preservation: preservation is stopping life to serve a future contingency; conservation is keeping life going. The union of powerful art and powerful nature into something beyond the sum of their separate powers deserves to be kept living. As the waterfall of Bear Run needed the house to enter the realm of art, so the joint work of art, Fallingwater in its setting, needed the Western Pennsylvania Conservancy to enter a new life of public service. I believe the happy coincidences that have marked this enterprise from the start will continue to favor its new existence in the hands of the Conservancy. I believe the Conservancy will give nature, the source, full due, and art, the human response to nature, full respect. For this confidence I am most grateful to Western Pennsylvania Conservancy and to the community that supports it so well.

Fallingwater in a New Role

As the transfer of Fallingwater was being planned, it seemed probable that the transition from private to public uses would be lengthy. I wanted to be on hand when needed, which happily the Conservancy has made possible.

66

The interesting and intricate story of the Conservancy's development of Fallingwater should be told by them. I recall that amid many uncertainties they took time settling in. The grounds staff were kept on, and their routines were relied on at first; my advice was sought in some matters of a general sort. The decisive influence, however, was the response of visitors who came in increasing numbers to see the house despite a remote location, a lack of public transportation in the area, and an entrance fee. To meet the needs of the public the Conservancy introduced basic facilities and routines. A small reception center was housed in the former gardener's cottage, and a supervised area for children too young to be taken on tour was set up in another cottage. At the house itself, visitors, led by guides, were toured in groups of a dozen or so; congestion was avoided in the narrow hallways, and questions could be answered; the guides set an agreeable and efficient tone for the Fallingwater experience. The Conservancy found guides among local residents, sometimes augmented in summer by students.

At the beginning of the Conservancy's ownership it was not clear how many visitors might be expected, nor what expenses would be, nor even what was prudent in the way of leaving or removing furnishings and decoration. Daily attendance grew until no more people could be properly toured through the house. The maximum in an eight-month season is about 70,000, and attendance has remained fairly near this level year after year. The time had come for the foundation to augment the endowment, for the Conservancy to establish regular procedures, and for the interior presentation to be much improved. In that last effort we were well advised by Joseph T. Butler, who had furnished and overseen three important house museums in the Hudson River valley.

Less visible but more necessary was the maintenance of Fallingwater's structure, undertaken by the Conservancy's on-site administrator Edward A. Robinson. The house needed freshening; the first step was to restore the original colors of concrete and steel. Then, the more serious deterioration of concrete, carelessly mixed, required long investigations. In 1976 it was decided to sandblast all the concrete, inside and out, before patching and repainting. Cleaning up the sand was an Augean task. This program was undertaken piecemeal to allow tours to continue. As mentioned, a thorough reworking of roofs and terraces and their flashing has been continued. Step by step the Conservancy has secured the integrity of Fallingwater's structure.

By the mid-1970s the Italian publication on Fallingwater was out of print; a new, more authoritative statement was needed. Donald Hoffmann, a respected architectural historian and art editor of the *Kansas City Star,* was invited to do broad research and to write and select illustrations for a new book. His result was felicitous, and new information made it widely

The barns of the Bear Run property. The near one, built as a dairy by my father, has been remodeled as a nature-study center by the Western Pennsylvania Conservancy.

useful. This important adjunct to Fallingwater appeared in 1978.

In Fallingwater's grounds, too, experience brought improvements. Thanks to the eminent landscape architect W.G. Swain, paths, parking areas, and plantings were well conceived and redundant features were eliminated, such as the outdoor swimming pool, cutting gardens, and greenhouses.

The 1500 acres assembled by my parents have been more than doubled, assuring a safer watershed for Bear Run; acquisitions were funded by the Kaufmann Foundation. A major portion of the total acreage lies across the main roadway from Fallingwater; there the Conservancy remodeled a large barn as a center for nature studies and walking tours through the unspoiled uplands.

The care of visitors has been improved in relation to their increasing numbers. Parking areas for cars and chartered buses were planted for shade and sited well out of view from Fallingwater. New paths lead from the car parks to the house, taking advantage of dramatic rock formations and the murmuring brook. Directional signs on the property (and along the highways) have uniform lettering based on a clear typeface, which contributes to a dignified presentation of Fallingwater. In 1980 the Kaufmann Foundation underwrote the construction of a new visitors' center located near the parking areas. The building was designed by Paul Mayén as a series of linked units dispersed in the woods, each one serving a different need. A central assembly area was surrounded by a child-care unit; toilets and telephones; a display illustrating the history of the area and the structure of Fallingwater; and a book and souvenir shop. All were elevated above ground cover, protecting it, and were lit by open sides and central clearstories giving varied light. Recently a decision was made

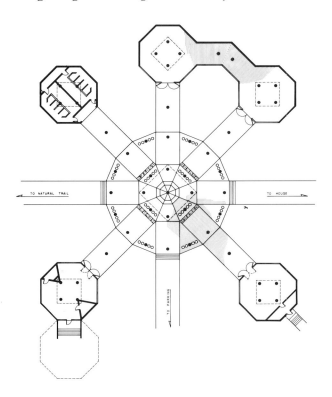

The Visitors' Center, built in 1979. The plan, reading clockwise from the lower left, shows a child-care area including outdoor playground; toilets and telephones; the restaurant with an informative exhibit on its walls; and the bookshop and souvenir store. One enters from the car park, below, and goes to Fallingwater on the righthand trail. To the left is a return path from the house. The photograph shows the restaurant area, and indicates that the whole structure is lifted lightly above ground cover.

70　The Visitors' Center, with steps leading to the trail to Fallingwater. BELOW: One panel of the informational exhibit in the restaurant; here, early days of the area are portrayed. OPPOSITE: The garage yard at Fallingwater with servants' bedrooms above. These now serve as offices for the Conservancy, while the garage has been enclosed as a lounge where the Conservancy's programs 'of which Fallingwater is only one) are presented in a slide lecture.

SCOUTS, SETTLERS, DEVELOPERS

to serve limited lunches, since there are no restaurants nearby. Located first in the former visitors' center, this service has been appreciated. It was enlarged and moved into the exhibition units of the new center.

House tours end in an upper garage court; here was an opportunity to tell the story of the Conservancy and its many programs. The open garages were remodeled into a comfortable lounge with a rear-projection screen presenting the message. The work was contrived to be removable without damage to the architecture. Membership in the Conservancy increased satisfactorily, and Fallingwater became further integrated with its operation.

As I see it, visitors come to Fallingwater for three main reasons: to satisfy ordinary curiosity, to see something rare and beautiful, and to explore Wright's architecture. They are permitted as much freedom as security and the attendance load permit. Those who want detailed information find it at the reception center, in the explanatory display there or, more fully, in the shop where a good selection of books is presented. Earnest researchers (often referred by universities, museums, libraries, and professional associations) are assisted. Foreign visitors, interested in Fallingwater's reputation as a distinctively American masterwork of architecture, are welcomed. And then concerts, other professional performances, and association meetings have been held on the grounds. These occasions are enhanced by special tours through the house, which, with room lights turned on for the evening, is magically transformed. All supplementary activities are, however, kept ancillary to the concept of serving a general public.

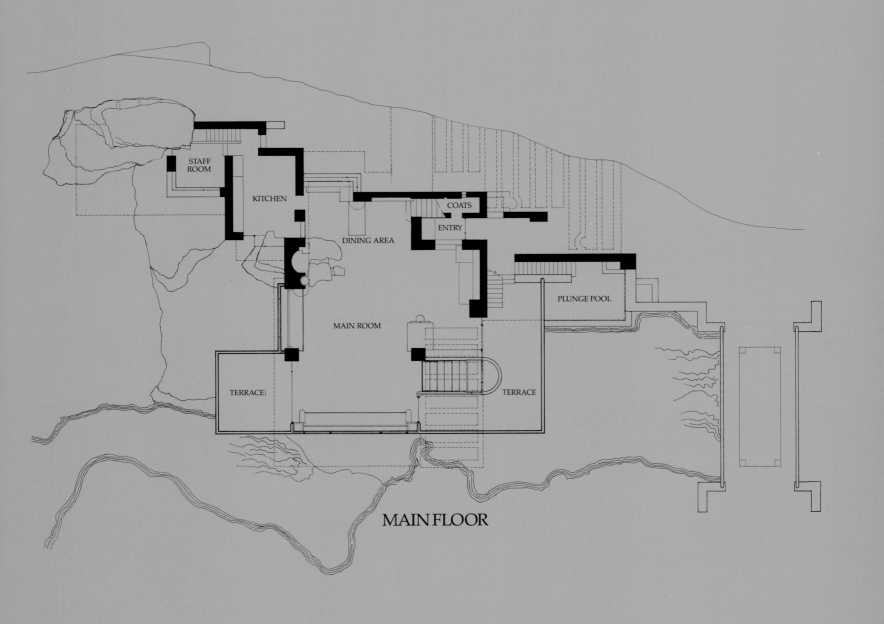

STAFF ROOM

KITCHEN

COATS

ENTRY

DINING AREA

MAIN ROOM

PLUNGE POOL

TERRACE

TERRACE

MAIN FLOOR

ENTRY AND
MAIN FLOOR

The driveway turns left at the end of the bridge, 77 passing under a trellis of reinforced concrete. This is the welcoming porte-cochere of Fallingwater, stretched from the house to the native cliff that defines the drive. Adjacent to this halting spot is the main door to the house, clear glass recessed within the stonework, drawing people into the inner spaces.

The main room at Fallingwater. *ABOVE*: Looking from the entry to the corner balcony over the falls. *LEFT*: Next to the entry, a record player cabinet adjoins a seat with high back panels. The Picasso print has been replaced with a more abstract work of art. The Chinese terracotta figurine was bought in Berlin in 1921. *RIGHT*: The large desk acts as anchor to the big room. It carries an African king, holding his heir; they face an early Japanese lacquer bowl, placed on a side table.

RIGHT: *An unusual view across the living room, from the east terrace toward the west. A French pottery figurine enjoys* vin du pays *while a cast-iron head of a Bodhisattva gazes at higher things. Similar iron heads were features of both Wright's homes; this was bought in emulation.*

Two views of the hatchway enclosing stairs from the living room down to the run. ABOVE: *A photograph showing how both sky and water are brought, simultaneously, into the house.* OPPOSITE, RIGHT: *Looking down on the trellis one can see that it is glazed over the living room and left open over the terrace.*

OVERLEAF: A furniture grouping next to the fireplace at Fallingwater. The fixed window looks down the glen. An upholstered bench has been placed at right angles to the built-in seat, and a fur throw has been folded over the bench. In the 1930s it was possible to make such throws of skins of various wild creatures native to the area; trappers were eager to sell them. But there are no more trappers, and the wildlife is undisturbed. Rugs and cushions add color to the scene.

The dining area at Fallingwater seats five but can be readily doubled by attaching a drop-leaf table that appears to be part of the buffet to the left. The chairs are traditional peasant seats found in Italy.

The kitchen looks out toward the view; to the left is the AGA stove, a skillfully engineered Swedish invention.

REALITIES AT
FALLINGWATER

What Fallingwater Is—and Is Not

In this sectional drawing, the two-story block of bathrooms seen on the upper right loads the lower floors' long cantilever over the stream; one weight counterbalances the other.

BELOW, RIGHT: The house is inserted between elements of the natural terrain. The relationship is harmonious, for a balancing of diverse forces is characteristic of both.

To understand Fallingwater one needs to explore its unusual structure, and Wright's reasons for designing it. The house may appear to consist of massive stone piers anchoring reinforced concrete projections, but this is misleadingly simple. Wright established a core, a sturdy stone-walled enclosure containing a kitchen and one bedroom above another, while also carrying flues, pipes, and wiring up to the various floors. Other stone walls, however, are divided into discontinuous segments—the concrete slabs continue intact right through the stonework. As the slabs extend outward, the pull on one side, in many places, counteracts the pull on the other. In addition, the main house is massed high at the back, and the accumulated weight counters the great projection over the stream. Thus Fallingwater utilizes and combines three kinds of cantilevering: extension from an anchorage (as in the iron arm suspending a kettle over the living room firegrate); counterbalancing (like simple scales); and loaded extension that permits limited anchorage (the way that a man squatting, with only the balls of his feet and toes touching the earth, extends his knees.) Another unobvious aspect of the construction is that each floor level has its own support system. The main level is carried on four inconspicuous stub walls rising at the edge of the stream bed; the slab extends far beyond them. The next level is supported from a central square of reinforced-concrete beams, with corners resting on stone masses; from this square the second slab, or tray, is cantilevered. The narrow top level is set along the rear edge of the house, bearing down on the whole.

Why did Wright design so complex a structure? Why was he so intent on cantilevering? I see Fallingwater as an irregular web of forces skillfully balanced to create floating horizontal levels. It is proper for such a structure to be inserted amid horizontal rock ledges naturally settled by similar adjustments

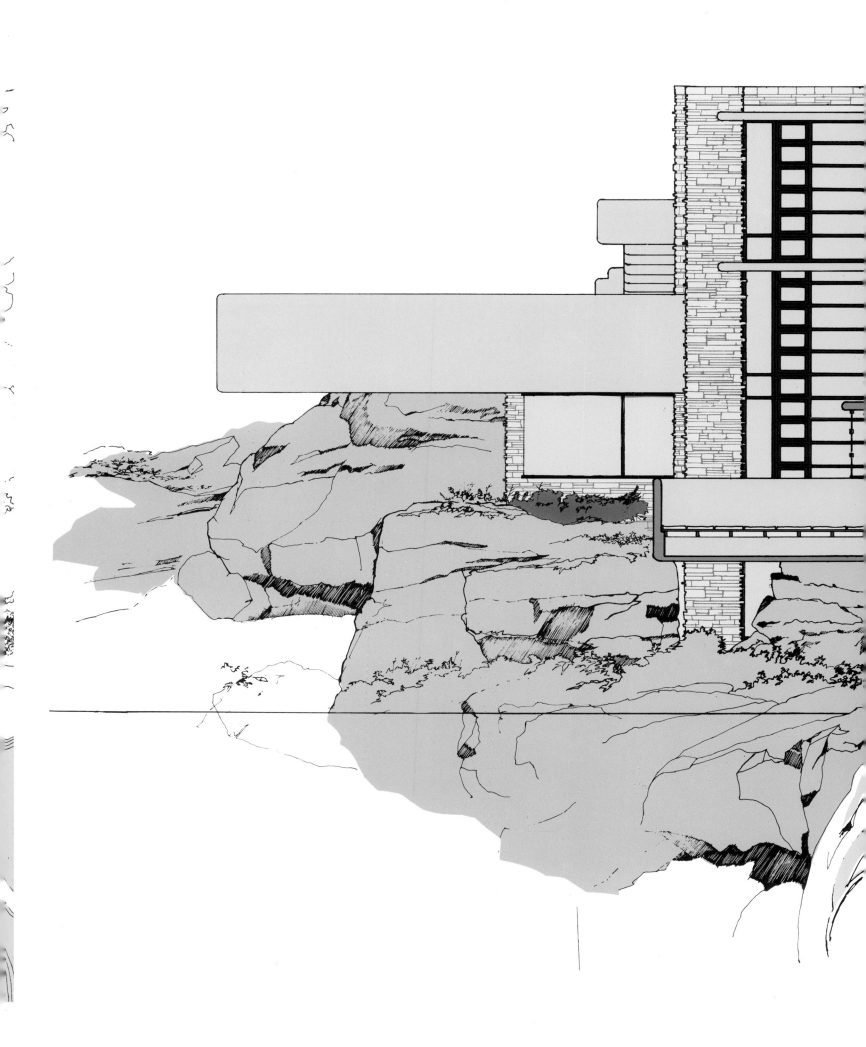

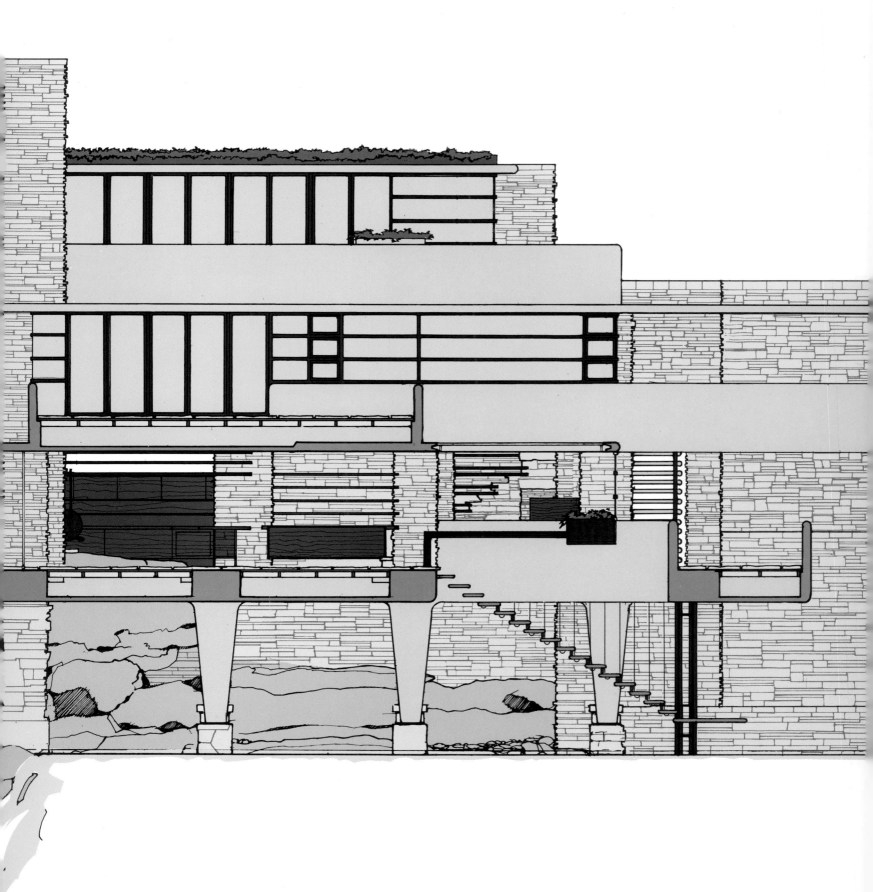

EAST–WEST SECTION

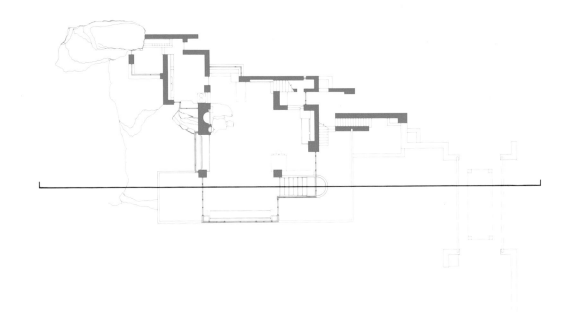

of forces. Moreover, cantilevering is a constituent feature of modern structural technology. For millennia building was dominated by uprights—posts or walls holding up beams, trusses, or vaults to provide shelter. Within the past two hundred years, however, a more scientific understanding of materials and forces gradually led (among several results) to horizontal constructions so strong in themselves that vertical supports can be greatly reduced in number and bulk. Furthermore, supports can be distributed freely between horizontal planes. This techological liberation gave rise to the "open plan" that has preoccupied all major creators of modern architecture, Wright in particular. His use of technology in the service of a humane architecture will be considered later.

It has been claimed that Fallingwater has flat roofs, ribbon windows, and unornamented surfaces—even pilotis—all derived from the International Style of modern architecture. Indeed, there are echoes of past and modern work in Wright's design; he willingly acknowledged that creative work requires precedents. However, at Fallingwater there are no ribbon windows; they appear to exist in some photographs and drawings only because upturned edges of slabs mask what lies behind them. Flat roofs, some used as livable terraces, have been common in many kinds of architecture. And, plain surfaces were evolved in Wright's work over decades as he learned to manage structure with a delicacy of touch that finally made decoration superfluous. Simplicity became typical of his buildings about the same time as avoidance of ornament began to be preached theoretically abroad; the trends converged from antithetical sources. Lastly, can one relate the modest stub walls underneath Fallingwater to Le Corbusier's demonstrative pilotis?

These misapprehensions of Fallingwater—touching its structure, its program, and its links to contemporary design—have led to much pointless analysis of the house, diverting attention from Wright's concept and his achievement.

Three petty misconceptions of Fallingwater should also be dispelled: that it is dedicated to Frank Lloyd Wright; that it exemplifies the 1930s; and that it is a museum of the arts. Each building by Wright is a memorial to his genius; Fallingwater was endowed and is operated as an example of this genius applied to the splendor of the Appalachians and to the life of a particular family. Numerous decades and cultures enliven Fallingwater with art and artifacts, and neither these supplements nor the house and its setting were meant to remain static—Fallingwater grew and still grows. It might not be far wrong to call Fallingwater an anti-museum, for it is rooted in the idea of living relationships, not in the storing of isolated treasures whether architectural or artistic. Fallingwater is dedicated to the values inherent in nature and in Wright's architecture, to my parents who made it happen, and above all to the visitors who enjoy it according to their various capacities.

The stub walls that support the main floor of Fallingwater, under construction at the edge of the stream.

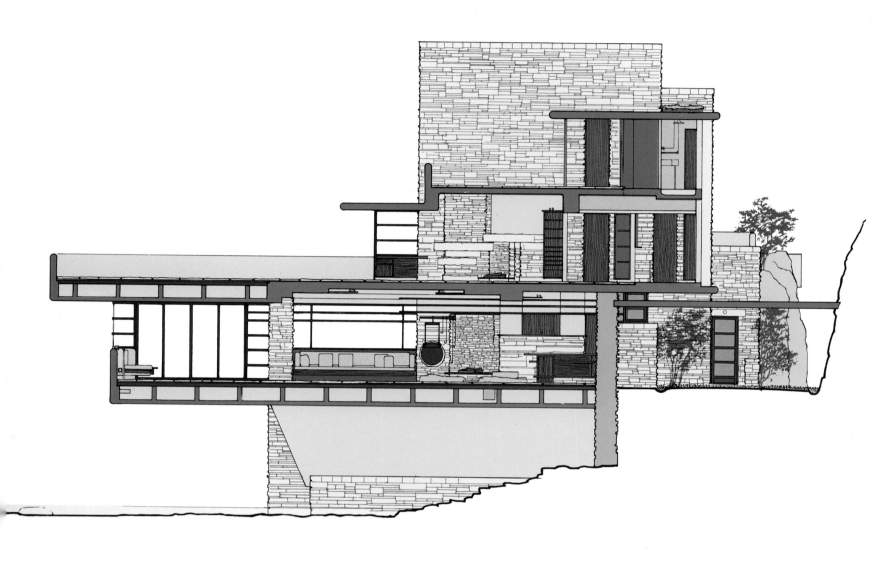

NORTH–SOUTH SECTION

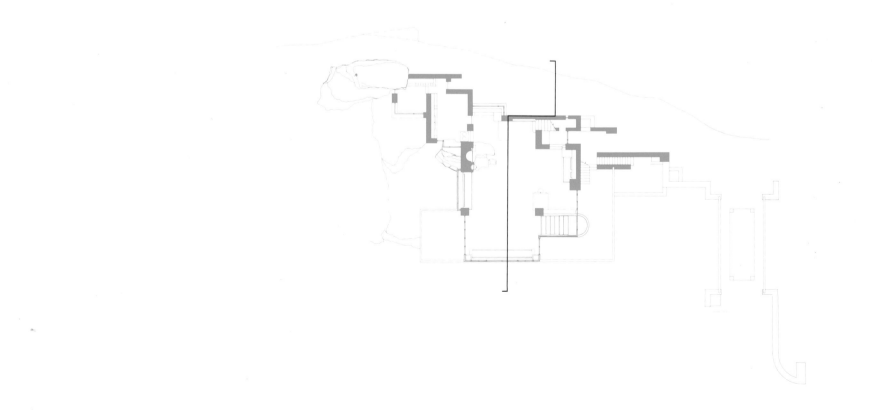

The Adaptability of Wright's Architecture

Wright's architectural procedures admitted adjustments readily; this can be appreciated by showing how he reacted to clients' requests for changes of design. For instance, at the main entry to Fallingwater Wright planned a small washroom under the stairs and a large cabinet for coats, etc., along the east stone wall of the living room. We thought that using the bathroom above, at the head of the stairs, would be convenient enough and less conspicuous. Why not put the coats under the stairs? Wright made no objection and provided, in lieu of the cabinet, a design for a Capehart record player with storage, and an upholstered seat and back. The back is exceptionally high, reaching up as far as the cabinet he had planned. The water for the washroom was turned outward, forming a jet at the doorway, for hand-rinsing after a ramble through the woods; the little pool that receives this jet had been a plant box.

The plunge pool below, at stream side, was requested for early morning dips, but this idea involved not the pool alone but steps leading down to it and further stairs going up outside to the bedrooms, so that water would not be tracked

OPPOSITE: At dusk the inside lighting makes clear the transparency of Fallingwater's structure on all sides except the back. The membrane of glass is no mere ribbon but varied to meet a variety of requirements.

A jet of water next to the front door welcomes all who enter with its cheerful plashing.

The approach side of Fallingwater displays Wright's virtuosity in controlling special details. The steps to the brook, skylit from above, remain dominant, while the stairs to the bedroom floor are quietly unobtrusive even though introduced within the structure at a late moment. From the lower terrace down to the plunge, stone stairs lie masked by the stone wall just left of the Lipchitz bronze.

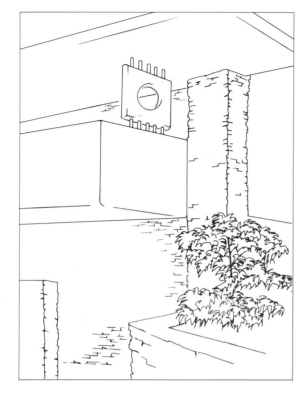

A sketch recreates my recollection of the design feature Wright placed above the entry to Fallingwater—of which no accurate record survives. This was replaced at the clients' request by a quieter support for the slab roof, and one stage in the process of simplification can be seen below. Eventually all the metal elements were eliminated, and only a stub of stonework was required for support.

OPPOSITE: At the eastern end of the third floor is an area intended to be opened to a bridge leading to the guest house above. When the bridge was built at the second floor this alcove became a bed space, and the room nearby became a study-dressing room; the third floor thus was turned into a commodious suite.

through the living room. This meant cutting through the upper terrace floor, already cast—all in all, a major operation that affected the character of a principal area of the house. Wright demurred but did not procrastinate; changes were discussed, designed, and built. A more purely esthetic change was requested for a feature supporting the roof over the same upper terrace. Wright's design seemed almost a heraldic device set over the entrance, not to our minds congruent with the rest of Fallingwater. Vertical steel straps joined the balcony parapet to the roof while a square of painted concrete overlapped them; a circular hole was opened in the square. We asked if a quieter treatment could be evolved. Plain vertical straps were tried, but the evident severity of this detail did not recommend it. At last a simple stub of stonework was built, which demonstrates the carrying of stone by reinforced concrete—just the system Wright was using throughout much of the house.

Later, the family asked for substantial changes when the guest and service wings were being designed. Cross ventilation was a necessity, since the master bedroom, below, had proved to be muggy during the still, hot nights of August. Like Wright, we were unwilling to consider air conditioning in the country; it would have separated indoors from out, definitively. At the start there was talk of sleeping on the terraces in bedsteads individually screened, but these contraptions were eliminated. The guest wing was built with a long clearstory window, which was opened from outside during the summer and closed wholly or in part the rest of the year.

Wright planned to connect the later structure to the top of the main house by a covered walk ending in a bridge; a spot had been provided for this juncture. Now we thought it would be more convenient to set the bridge one level lower down, where a suitable blank wall could be pierced. This passage has worked suavely (though the joint with the main house has been a source of leaks). Wright designed an additional section of the walk and its curved canopy, facilitating the change. The unused corner upstairs was appropriated for my bed; there I could enjoy the morning sun. The bedroom became a study and dressing room. With Wright's approval I added bookshelves to this room like those on the stairs leading up to it; other book space in the house was fairly limited.

These complex data are not in themselves significant, but they show how Wright's system of design enabled him to make unanticipated accommodations without the loss of spatial clarity or structural integrity. He went beyond open plan —in the sense of floor plan alone—into fully three-dimensional open design. This let him exploit the limitations of a commission—whether due to site, materials, budget, or people—with unexampled freedom. He used this freedom to create an individual architecture attuned to its environment and to the living habits of his clients.

The bridge across the driveway, seen from above.

OPPOSITE: Wright's original suggestion for lamps to be used throughout Fallingwater. A floor lamp, table lamp, and wall fixture were sketched. A far quieter system of built-in lighting was used, supplemented by a few table lamps of exceptional and elegant simplicity.

What we wanted at Fallingwater was neither lordly stateliness nor a mimicry of frontier hardihood, but a good place for city people to renew themselves in nature. A bipolar life was not overly familiar to Wright, and he suggested some details more fitted to a different program. For example, from his Japanese experience, he considered gold leaf on the concrete, inside and out, or paint with gleaming mica particles. Either would have been alien to our easy-going country life. He proposed great lamps, lighting the living room at night, but they introduced an odd solemnity. Specially designed carpeting through the main room would have been too luxurious and would have differentiated the interior too strongly from the terraces and grounds outside. Avoiding such features we could live relaxedly in harmony with Wright's design, including his sparely elegant furnishings, built-in and movable; only a few changes and supplements were needed. Wright accepted them, making minor alterations when he came to see us. In these ways, Fallingwater was indubitably his and indubitably ours.

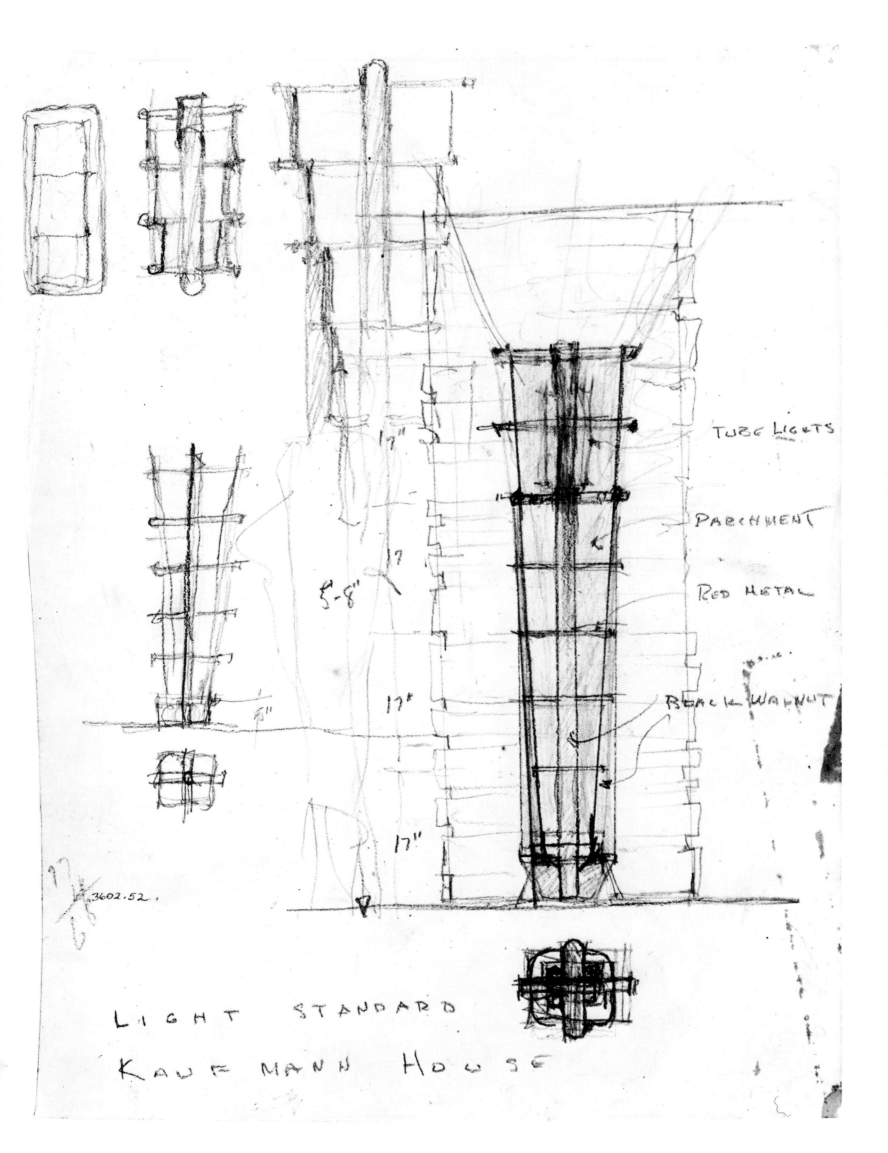

TUBE LIGHTS

PARCHMENT

RED METAL

BLACK WALNUT

5-8"

17"

17"

17"

3602.52.

LIGHT STANDARD

KAUFMANN HOUSE

Wright's Systems—and Mutations

Wright, as described earlier, found freedom of construction and planning in cantilevered forms, especially those made of reinforced concrete. In this material steel rods join with cement and gravel, hardening into an amalgam of great strength, if properly fabricated. The cantilevered, horizontal elements of Fallingwater were cast in reinforced concrete and finished with a coat of matte, sandy, warm-tinted paint. Where necessary, the slabs were cast with extra rods and concrete, forming integral beams. The slabs may be considered in two ways, as floors and as ceilings. Floors are level, with upturned edges (parapets) that give extra rigidity to the horizontal planes, just as the sides of a cardboard box make it stronger than a flat sheet would be. Lifted above the floor slabs by thin ribs of concrete lies a layer of redwood covered with roofing paper and loose sand to receive rippled flagstone quarried on the property, as is all the stone used. Air space between slab and redwood acts as insulation. Ceilings are also cast in reinforced concrete, strengthened by folding, which gives a stepped appearance. Naturally, some slabs act as both ceilings (below) and floors (above), as the drawings indicate. Reinforced concrete that permits cantilevering is the primary material of Fallingwater.

The next most important material is stone. Stone walls serve to space concrete slabs the proper distance apart, and prevent them from twisting. The native stone is laid up in distinct layers, irregularly projecting on all sides. On one occasion the rough stone indoors led a lady visitor to ask my mother, after due compliments, "Tell me, Mrs. Kaufmann, how will you get the wallpaper to stick on these walls?" Stone walls are left untreated, but within the house the stone flooring is waxed for cleanliness, becoming shiny. Yet stone walls and floors unite in contrast to the cement, inside and out.

OPPOSITE, ABOVE: The concrete slab for the main floor shows the structure of the hatchway to the brook, as well as the ribs over which stone flagging was laid on redwood boards; workers apply surface finish to the parapet of a concrete overhang.
OPPOSITE, BELOW: A local mason trained in Wright's methods lays up a stone wall, guided by the irregular layering that occurs naturally in cliffs on the property, seen on the right.

BELOW: To create extra rigidity, reinforced concrete slabs are folded, a device Wright used in several variations throughout the structure of Fallingwater.

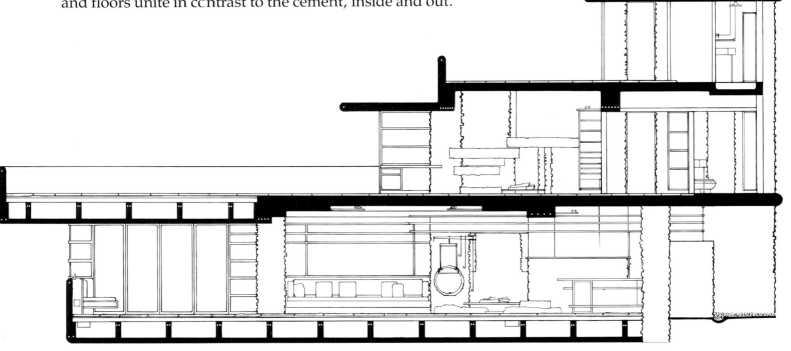

110

Horizontal window frames in Fallingwater extend outward as long, narrow shelves in several places.
ABOVE: *In the bathroom of the main bedroom, metal frames receive wood shelves to hold objects and plants, curtaining the bath.*
BELOW, RIGHT: *The framing of the clearstory window in the dining area changes into protruding shelves with thickened edges that continue to the right into shelves of walnut.*

OPPOSITE: *The great three-story glass wall, the western feature of Fallingwater. Without screens the windows open to show that no corner post is necessary. The concrete floors of the house are beveled to meet the slender horizontal frames, allowing the sheer curtain wall to continue uninterrupted.*

The structure arising from the union of the two materials creates spaces for living but does not shield them from the weather. That duty is assigned to a vertical membrane of glass held in a framework of steel, painted earth red. These frames were made to order from stock sections by Hope's, a well-known firm. Glass panels that open for passage or ventilation join with fixed glass in a continuous glazing membrane. This is the third element of the house; nothing more is required for shelter.

Wright used only a few elements throughout the house, so that a sense of familiarity soon reassures whoever visits or inhabits it. However, Wright was never content with consistency; he structured the whole western tower block using mutations of his themes. Supported on three sides by stone walls, the floor slabs of this portion of the house do not have parapets. On the contrary they are beveled to meet, but not pierce, the glazing membrane that here—and only here at Fallingwater—becomes a vertical curtain three stories high. This sheer expanse of glass and steel is not treated as a flat façade but is stepped forward in accord with the angled character of the house. Extending westward from this block is a cantilevered terrace not level with the floor slabs to the east, making clear that the tower interrupts the continuity of the reinforced slab system. The special treatment of the west end of the house is balanced to the east by another mutation: the concrete slabs repeatedly slotted to form the trellis areas over the driveway and the living room.

Wright's play of systems and mutations enlivening the architecture of Fallingwater is sometimes less emphatic than in these east–west features. For instance, as the house is set back floor by floor in accord with the sloping terrain, the glazing membrane is skillfully varied. Around the living room the membrane is extended continuously on three sides with no vertical posts delineating corners. Four separate elements augment it: the glass entrance door, a fixed glass panel next to the chimney, a clearstory light over the buffet adjoining the dining

Wright created long, drawn-out lines and planes to achieve repose amid daring structural exploits, and his use of trellises over the eastern terrace and driveway balances the three-story glass wall on the west.

table, and the glazed panels of the overhead trellis. At the main bedroom level the same system is set around the master bedroom and bath and the small guest room, but the whole expanse is reduced and simplified. At the top there is a clear run of glass, half of it floor to ceiling.

Uphill, the guest wing, set on leveled ground, echoes many of the themes introduced in the main house. The bravura of the glass curtain wall of the west tower is matched by a curved, repeatedly stepped (i.e., folded) canopy over the walk. The canopy rises from the rear of the main house and circles around a big oak tree until it meets the upper structure. This bold canopy is supported by steel posts on only one side; on the other, the tension created by a ring beam with additional reinforcing rods prevents the slab from sinking—a true *tour de force*. The canopy continues straight eastward along the front of the guest wing to form a trellis echoing those below; this trellis includes the longest cantilever of the whole house, very quietly presented. The glazing membrane is still further diminished at this level, continuing the sequence observed on lower floors.

The long front wall of the guest wing has embedded in it a number of steel posts covered with lath and cement plaster painted to merge with the concrete. Typically, Wright was not concerned to express the skeletal structure but rather to build expediently, achieving a harmonious whole that was understandable but not explicit. Similar plaster walls (without steel posts) enclose bathrooms at the rear of the main house and define the master bedroom and bath and the small guest room and its bath within the interior. Surprisingly, plaster covers portions of the stone walls next to fireplaces in the main bedroom and in the big living room. These are not true mutations but small deviations from Wright's systematic approach. In this very area of the living room, the metal framework of the glazing membrane is extended far beyond the glass; the horizontal bars mutate into shelves that wrap around the interior corner and curve out to meet a stone wall. Further shelves of wood continue the theme. This play of horizontals distracts attention from the anomalous wall treatment and strongly ties the corner elements together.

The guest wing restates design themes and details used in the main structure. Stairs leading to the servants' rooms are similar to those on the western terrace built two years earlier.

OPPOSITE: *The long front of the guest wing lies between a flagged terrace and a cantilevered slab pierced to create a trellis at the east end.*

Presenting Continuous Space

Wright asserted that "an architect's limitations are his best friends"; if so, at Bear Run he found a most friendly site! To interweave the geotechtonic dynamism of this terrain with the tensile energies of cantilevered construction was a full-scale architectural enterprise. But Wright also main-

114

tained throughout his design a poetry of repose, assuring renewal of the human spirit in nature. The Bear Run area in itself is an image of renewal, a territory pretty well ravaged years ago by timbering and surface coal mining, one that had regained its natural qualities gradually and with gentle newness. To keep the setting unscathed while fostering a serene way of living—there was Wright's challenge. The usual parade of house–terrace–garden–grounds would not serve; something more supple and integrated was called for. Wright had been working in this sense for forty years. He knew the resources at his command as an experienced craftsman does, but as an artist he aimed to go beyond experience into the potential he intuited. Almost every room in the house is continued outside, reaching freely into nature without infringement. The cantilevered terraces of Fallingwater may be luxuries, but they are necessary to the quality of life that was lived there.

At Fallingwater Wright, as was his wont, eliminated changes between in and out: stone walls maintain their texture on all sides; floor levels continue without thresholds; low ceilings step down even lower (some hallways are only six feet four inches high) and continue evenly into the flat eaves, guiding one's attention to the real protagonist of Wright's design: nature. As a result, the variations of natural light and seasonal progressions in plants and atmosphere become the chief enliveners of Fallingwater; decorations within are ancillary. When the drawings for the house were being reviewed and refinements were introduced, like the wood subfloors that could deaden sound, Wright kept emphasizing this aspect of his design, the continuity of space—inside and out all one— and the parallel continuity of material elements—floors, walls, ceilings—whether inside or out. My father was enthused by this concept; looking at the glazing design he asked about vertical metal members meant to hold glass against

The balcony over the falls is the key to the organization of Fallingwater; indoor and outdoor space unite. Stone flagging uninterrupted by thresholds extends from the entryway to the tip of this balcony.

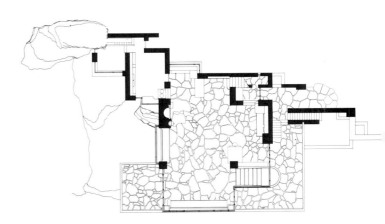

118

BELOW AND RIGHT: The superb stonework of Fallingwater receives glass and concrete with apparently effortless ease. This textured mass unites the space of the stairwell and offers a foil to special features that identify each floor level.

OPPOSITE: The living room before and after completion of interior details and furnishings. Incandescent bulbs first used were too large to fit above the translucent shield Wright designed, but fluorescent tubes are entirely effective alternates.

rough piers of stone; were they not awkward? Wright agreed, and the device successfully adopted at Fallingwater was to run glass with its horizontal dividers into a caulked recess in the stonework. The stone appears uninterrupted by glazing.

Frank Lloyd Wright's desire to present continuous space influenced the lighting of Fallingwater. The glazed membrane remains almost entirely without curtains or blinds, and daylight enters unhindered. The seclusion of the site provides privacy (a small guest room, the kitchen, and the servants' quarters do have wood-slatted venetian blinds). Because of the abundant daylight, certain pictures and textiles affected by light can be used only in sheltered positions.

At night the electric light within extends freely outward, and the whole house acts as a great lantern in the forest, giving shape to the dark. Outdoor lighting destroys this close relationship of house and grounds; once tried it was quickly abandoned.

Wright usually liked to integrate electric lighting with his architecture, avoiding lamps, even though reading and writing required them. He designed one—in four versions, large and small, horizontal and vertical—with walnut shields pivoting to allow directed light. For general illumination Wright, as he had often done before, planned shielded light strips atop

cabinets; light was reflected from the ceilings. This arrangement could be made more compact with fluorescent tubes, then newly available in sizes suited to residential needs. I suggested placing such strip lighting along the backs of fixed seating; this increased overall illumination and cast light out through glass to the eaves. It was another way to show the unity of structure indoors and out.

Fluorescent tubes available in the mid-1930s gave a cold light, but reflected from a warm-tinted ceiling the result was acceptable. Fluorescents were also used in the recessed ceiling fixtures Wright designed for the main room. The light was to have been shaded by Japanese paper, but since this was not available in large-enough sheets unbleached muslin serves as a satisfactory substitute. One ceiling fixture edges a beam, lighting the dining alcove; adjoining it an open square of lighting ornaments the central space of the room. The fixtures distract attention from the heavy concrete beams, which incidentally, are so formed that incandescent lamp bulbs, originally installed, would have scorched either paper or cloth. Happily the introduction of fluorescent tubes resolved that difficulty.

At first, interior lighting seemed insufficient; Wright proposed various designs for lamps, but none seemed to fit in gracefully. Floor cavities throwing light upward were considered but rejected as impossible to shield adequately. In time, however, improved fluorescents and a strong down light over the desk gave the living room agreeable, useful lighting.

Fallingwater in Its Setting

The man-made parts of Fallingwater would be incomplete without the natural setting; the interaction of site and building is more intricate and meaningful at Fallingwater than appears at first sight. From downstream the concrete parapets of the house seem to sublimate the great native rock ledges, echoing, completing, and ordering them. House and rock relate in other ways already indicated: the cliff face of the driveway becomes part of the entry. Layered stone outcroppings are features of the terrain, their character echoes in the stone walls of the house and in the rippled flagging that covers its floors. Large boulders enter into the structure of Fallingwater. The western terrace is anchored in one, and others occur inside service areas, also at the west end. The most prominently intrusive boulder appears as the living room hearth. It has been said that Wright may have intended to cut its top down level with the floor, and that my father suggested it be left intact. To see how unlikely this is one must think of the cut-

TOP: *Light set behind shields on the top of the built-in seating is thrown up to the ceiling, so that the glass seems to disappear.*

ABOVE: *Reading and writing required task lights, and, after some searching, Wright designed the simple lamp stand pictured here, with its pivoting shade to adjust the light. The cast iron base, finished in matte dark brown, holds a walnut veneer shade painted inside with reflective aluminum. The same lamp stand is used with a longer shade, or with upright shades, long or short, according to need.*

OPPOSITE: *Fallingwater at night seems to float in the glen. Trellises everywhere are enlivened with small points of light, built in.*

OVERLEAF: *Boulders and cliffs on the site accent the architecture, so that the work of mankind merges with nature.*

From the west, Fallingwater is linked to native features: cliff and boulder.

The boulder top serving as hearth in the main room is a reminder of omnipresent nature.

At the end of the bridge across the driveway, the rough cliff face accents the interior.

off surface amid the rippled flagstones, an incredible juxtaposition.

Water and building repeatedly conjoin, first of all at the extension of the living room balcony over the falls. There the house hovers over the running stream—two elements in harmony. Were the house to reach down across the brook for support, Bear Run would be caught within the architecture (like Ledoux's image of the river Loue). Running water spouts out cheerfully at the entryway and again pours into the tranquil plunge pool at the east end of the house. So it does also at the guest house up the hill in another plunge pool, encircled by concrete walls. The sound of running water permeates the air of Fallingwater.

Trees, too, interweave with the design of the house, slender verticals accenting the bold concrete parapets. A large tulip poplar became a feature of the entrance trellis; after maturity it died and a replacement was planted. Furthermore, some saplings were meant to rise through the western terrace, but they did not survive the rigors of contruction work.

The major relationship of the house and site arises from setting the building within the valley. Wright placed the structure close to the falls and to its underlying rock fault. He was following the Kaufmann family's feeling that the falls was the heart of their property and of their attachment to it. At the same time he was following his own sense of the challenge posed by this fault, a break that called for the healing presence of architecture. By setting the house deep in the declivity Wright was assuring its integration with the natural features; lifting it higher would evoke feelings of dominance and separation. But this closeness severely limited the area where footings could be set for the structure, only a narrow strip of land was available between the stream and cliff to the north. An old road, built for logging, lay along this strip, and a small, strong, wooden bridge crossed the run. However, this narrow area allowed a favorable orientation of the building, and the bridge, properly set at right angles to the flow of water, indicated the basic axes of a future structure. Wright often had been attracted by steep, problematic sites, and here was one that could be developed with cantilevering; the whole house could rise almost spontaneously out of the setting, thanks to a bold technology. For Wright this was a natural.

The precise relationship of floor levels to ground was crucial in such a floating structure, and Wright assessed the limitations imposed by large boulders indicated on the topographic survey he had received. As mentioned, one tall and sturdy rock appealed to him; it lay amid a daunting tangle of trees, shrubs, and vines, rising from a steep slope, practically inaccessible. Wright appreciated that it would serve as the center point of the house. Even absorbed into Fallingwater as it now is, the boulder top, rising unaltered above the floor, emanates a dense and powerful air of nature in the raw.

C.-N. Ledoux's image of the picturesque river Loue carried through a structure to measure and control its flow; nature is trapped in architecture.

OPPOSITE, ABOVE: Trees were received into the architecture of Fallingwater, but, alas, the small saplings did not survive the rough treatment of construction work.
OPPOSITE, BELOW: The bridge designed as a gate to Fallingwater is set where the timber structure serving loggers used to stand. The old ccttage up the hill stood where now the guest wing extends its length.

In all these ways Fallingwater responds to, and integrates with, the natural setting. Furthermore, there are practically no gardens or special plantings; nature is the garden.

Inside Fallingwater

Frank Lloyd Wright's furniture set the tone of Fallingwater's interiors. It was veneered in black American walnut, retaining the sapwood; flitches were applied lengthwise over doors, table tops, and banks of cabinets. Thus room doors are striated vertically and rows of cabinets horizontally—in treatment somewhat like the glass membrane, where most openable units are framed vertically, and fixed ones horizontally. The system of woodwork at Fallingwater includes not only cabinets and shelves, but also tables and desks; the last often contain radiators. Fixed wooden headboards are part of this system and may extend into bedstands. Bedroom storage cabinets are designed in typical Wright fashion—their tops continue as thin shelves forming recesses for doors; cabinets and doors are closely related. The shelf-top carries the light strip and also affects the space of a bedroom, giving it variety and movement.

Major features in the living rooms at the main house and the guest wing are long seats built along exterior walls, cantilevered just above the floor, and edged with walnut front rails.

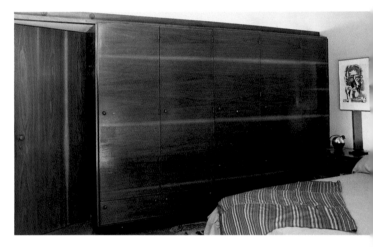

OPPOSITE: Fallingwater is set low in the glen, just above the rock ledges, assuring it integration with nature, its garden. 127

LEFT AND ABOVE: The built-in furniture, veneered in black walnut, is actively engaged with masonry and glass elements: desk tops are cut back to allow windows to open, and veneers that retain lighter sap streaks mark upright doors and broad sequences of storage closets. The same contrast of horizontals and verticals indicates fixed or movable areas of glass.

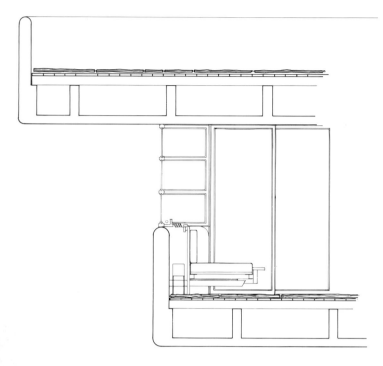

This section drawing shows how built-in seats serve to direct air over the radiators, and to throw light up to the ceiling and eaves outside.
BELOW: Wright-designed furniture in the living room includes built-in benches and stools both high and low—all upholstered in latex foam. They are veneered in walnut.

Seats and backs were upholstered with latex foam, newly available then in the United States; it still serves after half-a-century of use. Behind these seats radiators and light fixtures were located.

Movable furniture, Wright-designed, complements the fixed units. Two kinds of backless square stools have latex upholstery; some occasional tables are long rectangles, others have square tops. The woodwork of all these is veneered in black walnut.

In his own homes Wright often used store-bought easy chairs, and at Fallingwater upholstered armchairs, designed by T. H. Robsjohn-Gibbings, slightly simplified, are set in the living room. At the dining table Wright recommended a barrel chair newly redesigned by him for the imposing S. C. Johnson residence outside Racine, Wisconsin. A model was made in walnut, but in our weekend house the form seemed stiff. A traditional Alpine chair was used instead. This has a dominant seat slab, into which three legs are inserted, and a slightly sloping back silhouetted in baroque curves. This peasant chair is far from Wrightian but suits the informal room. In the bedrooms diverse chairs are used, most of them designed by well-known contemporaries, friends from my days at the Museum of Modern Art. Finn Juhl, Bruno Mathsson, Josef Frank, and

Jorge Hardoy come to mind, as does a regular weekend guest at the house, Laszlo Gabor. In the upper guest bedroom there is a boldly turned Victorian easy chair from the Washington Irving house; it became available when the house was restored as Irving lived in it. Outdoor furniture, much of it from Van Keppel-Green of California, had the frames painted in earth red like the window frames. All these items increase the personal character of the furnishings yet do not disrupt the basic tone set by Wright. He did not object to them, but he balked at some tree trunks used upside down as chair-side tables—the inversion disturbed him.

Textiles enliven Fallingwater's rooms. The long, built-in seats, originally covered in beige monk's cloth, now have an equally reticent but sturdier fabric. In contrast, low stools and some loose back cushions on the long seats are covered in clear, unfigured red or yellow. To them are added variegated pillows. Throws and hangings, informally figured and colored, are freely disposed, and most important of all are the spirited rugs, products of folk craft from many countries.

With these colorful accents a new aspect of Fallingwater becomes clear. The textiles, the chairs, other minor but numerous decorative objects, and the paintings, graphics, and sculpture are free variations set against the primary systems

BELOW, LEFT: The slender barrel chair Wright proposed for the dining area seemed static when grouped and was not adopted. However, the sample, set at a guest-room desk, appears graceful.
BELOW: Ancient peasant chairs from Italy, placed around the dining table, add liveliness. Inverted stumps used as chairside tables irritated Wright, but to the family they recalled native chestnut trees lost in a widespread blight.

Three details of furnishing, from living room, bedroom, and kitchen.

established by Wright—the systems of concrete, stone, glazing, lighting, and woodwork. The variations were left to the inhabitants, and at Fallingwater this meant my mother first of all. She was well-prepared to follow Wright's lead, her wideranging taste and keen attention allowed her to improvise with grace and individuality. That such collaboration was sought by Wright is clear enough; in his own homes he eagerly assembled and placed works of art and products of craftsmanship, mostly of Oriental origin. These were supplemented by arrangements of greenery and flowers. The wealth of incidental accents led to constant play and experiment that Wright thoroughly enjoyed. Moreover, he urged apprentices at Taliesin to practice their skills in the same manner; the duty of decorating interiors with temporary greenery and other accessories was regularly assigned and the results appraised as part of the architectural training. An ingenious arrangement was not as prized as one that harmonized with the character of the architecture in which it was set. At Fallingwater this exercise, whose results are as evanescent as morning dew, is continued to this day.

When the Conservancy introduced guided tours it became necessary to eliminate some interior furnishings and to provide certain safeguards, but maintaining the residential character of the house has been a constant ideal. Inspired by color illustrations in the Italian publication that show the house as occupied by the family, fresh flowers are used throughout. The dining table is set, a bed is turned down to show the special linens, closets are opened to view in a bedroom and in the kitchen. The kitchen has its original fittings, although the Swedish AGA stove is not exactly like the one installed at first; however, our interest in efficient fuel consumption and temperature control is made evident. Walnut veneers, sadly deteriorated, are being restored. The many shelves and tables Wright provided throughout the house are enlivened by ornaments, the originals as far as possible, and by fresh books and magazines. Outdoor furniture has been reintroduced. Pictures and sculpture are treated in keeping with modern conservation practices. And, not least important, the rugs, bedspreads, upholstery, and other textiles that add color everywhere, are restored or replaced. This manysided program was evolved over the years and requires continuing attention; it is a slight but essential contribution to the vital character of Fallingwater.

Two views of a bathroom: the Kohler fixtures are finished in a warm beige enamel; mirrors above basins have frosted bands to illuminate faces, and glass shelves. Toilets are set low to ensure easy use; behind the toilet is an outlet for heating.

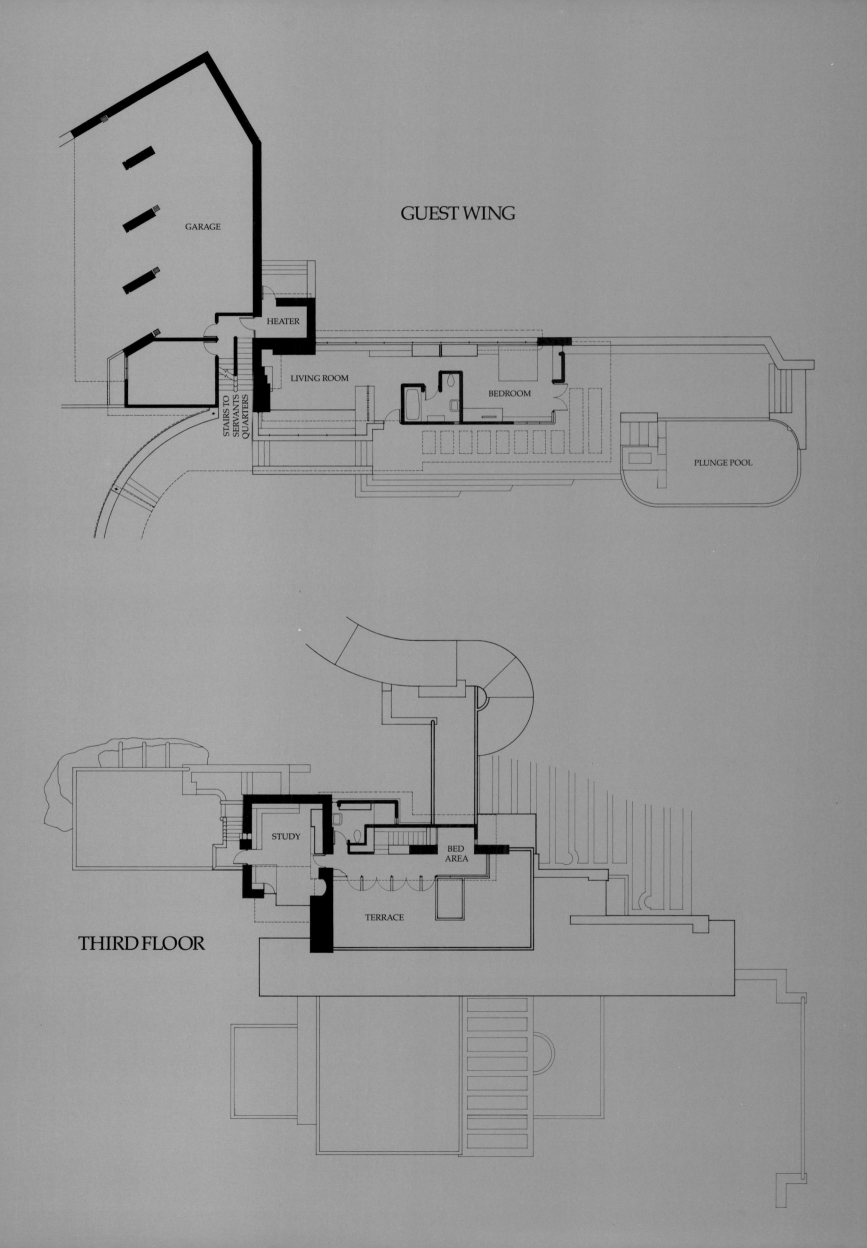

GUEST WING

GARAGE

HEATER

LIVING ROOM

STAIRS TO SERVANTS QUARTERS

BEDROOM

PLUNGE POOL

THIRD FLOOR

STUDY

BED AREA

TERRACE

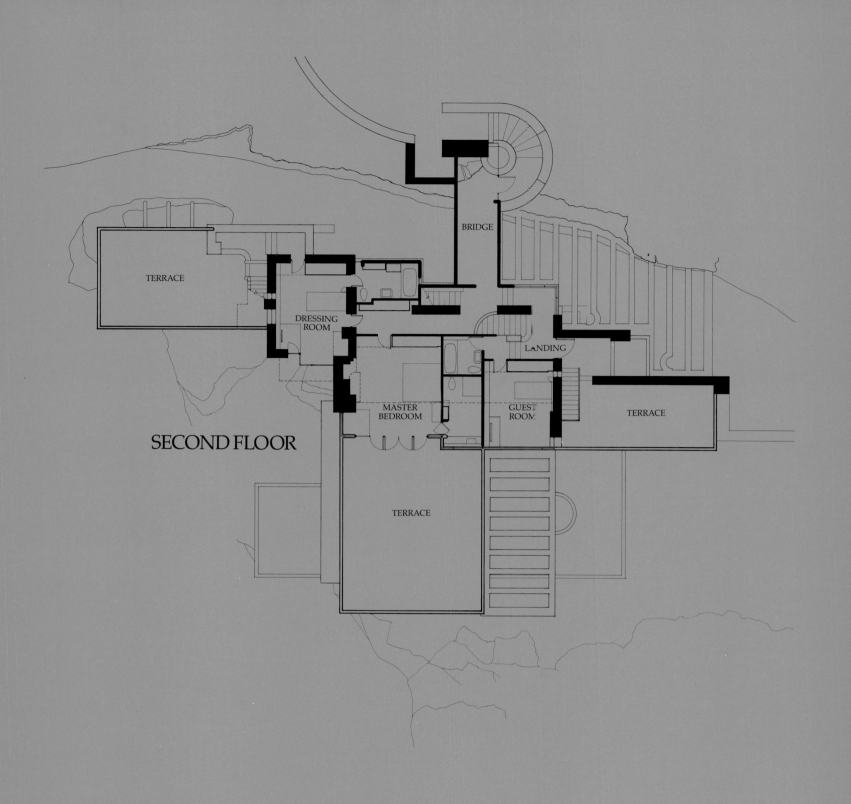

TERRACE

BRIDGE

DRESSING
ROOM

LANDING

SECOND FLOOR

MASTER
BEDROOM

GUEST
ROOM

TERRACE

TERRACE

UPPER FLOORS
AND GUEST WING

The second floor landing: steps on the left lead to a small guest room; at the center is a glimpse of the hallway to the main bedrooms; to the right are stairs to the third floor suite.

RIGHT: The desk in the master bedroom and its view of the glen. The peasant chair is English, the adjustable mirror Regency, and the lamp Tiffany. The lamp shade is ingeniously strengthened by folding (as are the large concrete slabs of Fallingwater).

OVERLEAF: From the terrace outside one can look into the main bedroom, space is continuous, as emphasized by the level floor without threshhold.

*Two views of the dressing room used
by my father. The leather sling chair by Ferrari-
Hardoy and his associates is one of the first to be
imported from Argentina; it was soon made in the
United States (under license) and widely copied.*

*OVERLEAF: The dressing room adjacent to the
main bedroom.*

The small guest room in the main house.

RIGHT: At dusk the transparency of the glass
membrane contrasts with the solidity of the
stonework.

Stairs leading up to the third floor are lined with bookshelves that Wright designed on request.

150 *The desk in the third-floor study. The marble sculpture is by Hans Arp.*

OVERLEAF: The window and fireplace of the third-floor study. The chair is by Finn Juhl of Copenhagen, a good friend.

*More views of the study: the red stone above the
fireplace was found in the quarry and set as a special
accent. The reclining chair is an early design by
Bruno Mathsson of Sweden. The books were donated
to the Conservancy by close friends and neighbors of
the family.*

OPPOSITE: *The third-floor gallery, looking from the
bed alcove toward the study.*

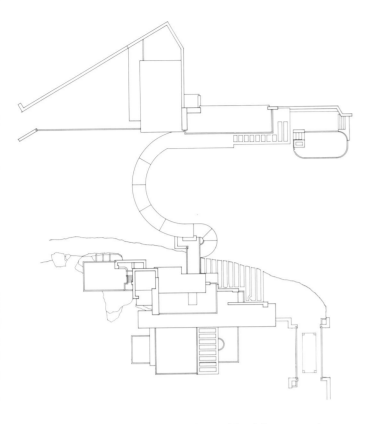

Plan showing the relationship of the guest wing to the main house.

RIGHT: Passageways at Fallingwater are kept in contact with nature. ABOVE: The curved, covered walk between main house and guest wing. One sees Wright's deft solution to bringing the bridge in at the second floor: he merely added a lower section of roof not attached to the old. This change was devised before construction. CENTER: A moss garden at the end of the bridge; glass divides the circular garden, half indoors, half out. Mossy rocks are found in the woods when the garden needs freshening. BELOW: A similar planted area is set over the main entrance.

OPPOSITE: The interior of the bridge over the driveway. Skylights above, natural cliff at left, and circular wall of moss garden to the right.

OVERLEAF: The stepped, reinforced-concrete canopy over the open walk from main house to guest wing. On the roof of the main house can be seen a long plant box that breaks the large surface of the roof seen from above.

The curved canopy over the walkway continues straight along the guest wing and ends in an east trellis like those below.

Looking from under the trellis one sees the plunge pool next to the guest bedroom.

RIGHT: Looking from the guests' plunge pool toward the wisteria-covered trellis. The large V-shaped tree is an old oak around which the curved walkway was swung.

The guest living room has some of the best stonework of Fallingwater. The long seat beneath the main windows can be made up as two beds if need be. The double bedroom for guests has an ample view and a plunge pool and paved terrace right at its door.

RIGHT: From the living room one looks along a bank of cabinets into the double bedroom. To the right a wood screen defines the entrance area from the seating. Since the wing is half buried in the hill, the clearstory windows lie just above ground level outdoors; they are opened from outside for ventilation as needed.

OVERLEAF: Looking out from under the guest wing trellis toward the big oak and the curving, stepped canopy that swings around it, leading down to the bridge to the main house, visible at far left. In the trellis one of the built-in lights appears, a slightly down-tapering pentagonal shape. The downward narrowing echoes the section through the trellis beams, but otherwise the shield shape is not repeated at Fallingwater.

IDEAS OF
FALLINGWATER

Images

Photoprints and films, in color and black and white, have made Fallingwater very widely known. In general they overdramatize cantilevering and ignore the serenity of the house. However, studious observers also look at the drawings (perspectives, elevations, plans, and sections) of the house made under Wright's direction; some are even his own work. Are these representations closer to Wright's concept of Fallingwater than the camera views? In some ways, yes. It is pertinent that Wright, who liked to use a camera, seems not to have taken photographs of his buildings. Nevertheless, Wright recorded his buildings in drawings of unusual skill. He enjoyed the procedures of drafting and trained his gifted assistants carefully, often retouching their drawings. These sheets were then displayed for pleasure and instruction in the studio or drafting room, and formed the basis of many books and exhibitions Wright organized. Despite this, Wright's graphic documents were generally mistreated; many were damaged by rough handling and by floods and fires that struck his offices from time to time. While demonstrating a point in architecture to his students Wright did not hesitate to reuse sketches, altering them at will. In this way I have seen furniture change into buildings and elevations into floor plans with a few flicks of the pencil. In short, Wright admired deft architectural drawings but treated them as aids to practice, not as precious end products. This is confirmed by his use of the fireproof vaults available at both his main homes. Treasured Japanese prints and screens, as well as important documents, were protected while most drawings of buildings were stored elsewhere, stacked on edge or laid flat on shelves in wooden cabinets. However, as Wright grew old he realized that the drawings made for his own use and that of clients and contractors were valuable records, worth saving for posterity and for the sheer monetary benefit of his estate after death. In the 1950s a new era of care was launched.

Another aspect of Wright's attitude toward drawings changed as time went on. At first Wright, like most architects, sketched variations of design; drawings survive that show how carefully he explored alternatives before making a choice. Gradually he was able to pursue such exploration in his own head, in imagination, before any sketch on paper. This was not just conceptual acrobatics, it fostered a fluid integration of space and structure and avoided the congealing inherent in the graphic act. This is what happened in the development of Fallingwater. When my father was due to arrive at Taliesin the basic sketches could be made rapidly, requiring only detailed alterations later, because Wright had been assimilating and coordinating the main elements of the house in the workshop of his mind.

OPPOSITE: Seen from an airplane, the house and its outlying wings spread through the forest.

Why was Wright so careless of drawings that recorded this rare form of creativity? Largely, no doubt, because he was focused on new activities. Wright might well have agreed with Sartre—a "quality . . . is given to every moment insofar as I am living in it . . . which it loses when I am living in it no longer." There may have been another reason. Along with his enjoyment of skilled draftsmanship Wright must have been keenly aware of the limitations of all graphic representations. As his architecture became more fully an art of spatial composition and immaterial values, mental imaging and refining would become essential. Drawings would not convey Wright's concept completely, for no graphic rendition, drawn by hand, seized in a lens, projected by laser or transmuted by computer, can convey such values.

What Images Do Not Tell

The spatial and immaterial values discussed earlier can be illustrated by tracing my own slow discovery of some recondite but powerful elements of Fallingwater's design. These are visible in drawings and photographs, but their actions and interactions are unlikely to be sensed until experienced on the site. To begin with, my father, in examining the plans, questioned the value of steps leading down from inside the living room to the stream. The water was shallow in this stretch, impractical for even a dip. The steps would be extravagant to build and would complicate the structure of the house. Granting this I felt that Wright wanted to keep the main room in touch with the movement and energy of the run, and I pleaded for trust in Wright's intuition. Wright himself considered the steps not so much a proposal as a decision. Eventually my father agreed and the steps were built. Only later I began to think about the steps in conjunction with the glazed trellis above them. Clearly Wright had gone to some length to achieve transparency along a vertical axis here; the eye could look down to the run and up to the sky. Diagonally across the room stood the great, solid chimney wall. I then saw the pair as a column of stone and a column of air marking a precinct, and was pleased with the discovery though ashamed of recognizing it tardily.

More years passed until I began to consider how unconventional a country house Fallingwater really is. A regular country house on ample acres would have a standard program in which outbuildings edge the approach, then a gateway announces the private domain (with implications of guards and challenges, a checkpoint) and in due course one reaches the entrance front, emphatically centered on the main door.

Fallingwater seems to reach out into nature, touching it gently. Stairs down to the brook emphasize this aspect of Wright's design; they keep the main room in touch with the running stream below.

LEFT: Just as the living room is kept in contact with the stream, the whole entry element of Fallingwater is so anchored into the cliff that the cliff is part of the architecture. This is Frank Lloyd Wright's initial statement to all who enter the house.

The bridge across the run, Fallingwater's gateway.

On one hand lie hospitable facilities, on the other, work areas of all sorts. Unseen but promised is a garden front, more open and relaxed than the approach façade. Wright sidestepped this whole program—or did he?

Our property had its outbuildings, none designed by Wright: caretaker's house, greenhouses, swimming pool, and lesser bits lining the drive. Today most of these have been eliminated in favor of parking areas and the visitors' center, dispersed among trees. The gateway–checkpoint at Fallingwater is the bridge across the run, where visitors must abruptly turn, gaining a first full view of the house. A second turn then leads under the driveway trellis. This is the formal entry, a generously proportioned porte-cochere (as well as a link between house and cliff and a structural necessity counterbalancing the east balcony). Once within the architecture, people and cars part; the cars, passing along the service area, are taken up to a garage. People are led in by a recessed, transparent door unless they choose to explore the remarkable entry front just passed. This is enriched with projections and recessions in concrete and stonework and outside stairs, with trees and plantings and spouts of water as well as the rock face along the drive. As you enter through the main door, your eye is drawn to the far corner of the interior, the south point of the house projected as a balcony right above the falls. Immediately

Fallingwater reaches out to Bear Run by projecting its south balcony over the falls. This is clearly seen from the base of the falls, where all upper elements of architecture fall into a coherent pattern centered on the prow of the balcony.

at hand, however, on the right, are the dining alcove, a kitchen door next to the large fireplace, and stairs leading up, visibly open to the entryway. On the left are seats and a broad desk flooded in daylight and more groups of seating disposed with views and features until the circling gaze again meets the fireplace.

Where is the garden front? At the falls! The south balcony, noted as one entered, when seen from the rocks at the foot of the falls, marks the center of this angled front. The house extends in strong horizontals to the right; to the left rises a stone-wrapped, glazed vertical shaft, a sturdy mast. This is the essential image of Fallingwater, the one best remembered. It is also the perspective chosen as background in Wright's color portrait on the cover of *Time* magazine. This perspective, Wright's choice, is set so that the outer corner of the south balcony lines up with an edge of the stone chimney pier, establishing a spine for a composition as rich as that of the approach front but more calm. Thus every canonical device of a conventional country house had its analog at Fallingwater.

The differences, however, are stronger than the similarities. For flat façades, here one must expect to see angular views; for each central motif, a corner feature. Wright has taken the conventions apart, sundered them as in a cubist drawing, but more consistently. The rectangular layout of the house, the house in utilitarian terms, is obvious in plan. But at another level of understanding one sees a diagonal pathway that leads from the fireplace with its native boulder hearth (earth and fire) to the skylit, open steps down to the brook (air and water). Thus the ancient cardinal elements lend sanction to the modern architect's statement. Crossing this pathway at right angles is a grand sweep of hospitality that begins in the shadowed, sunken entryway, extends through the expanse of living room, and goes beyond the south balcony into a widening forest vista down the glen—to the accompaniment of the falls. These two diagonal, virtual pathways establish the character of Fallingwater.

It is worthwhile, now, to examine Wright's earliest surviving sketch for Fallingwater, a rough draft in colored pencils, which shows the floor plans of each level in different colorings, drawn one over the other. This exploratory sketch, not meant for use outside the studio, indicates the irregular bays of the building. Furthermore, Wright set the plan diagonally on the paper, even though there was no earlier sketch on it. He conceived the house on angle, as he had done with many earlier designs. What led Wright to these angled conceptions? For a structure to have body and not merely be implied behind screening façades, it must protrude toward the observer (as the pyramid builders of Egypt already knew).

OVERLEAF: The first surviving sketch Wright made **175** *of Fallingwater. He had the complete concept of its extraordinary structure and its resonant composition so firmly in mind that only slight changes were needed later, as the building developed.*

The long bench built beneath the southeast windows of the living room. The near slope outside is thick with native rhododendron and a few trees; these are framed rhythmically, forming a decorative screen.

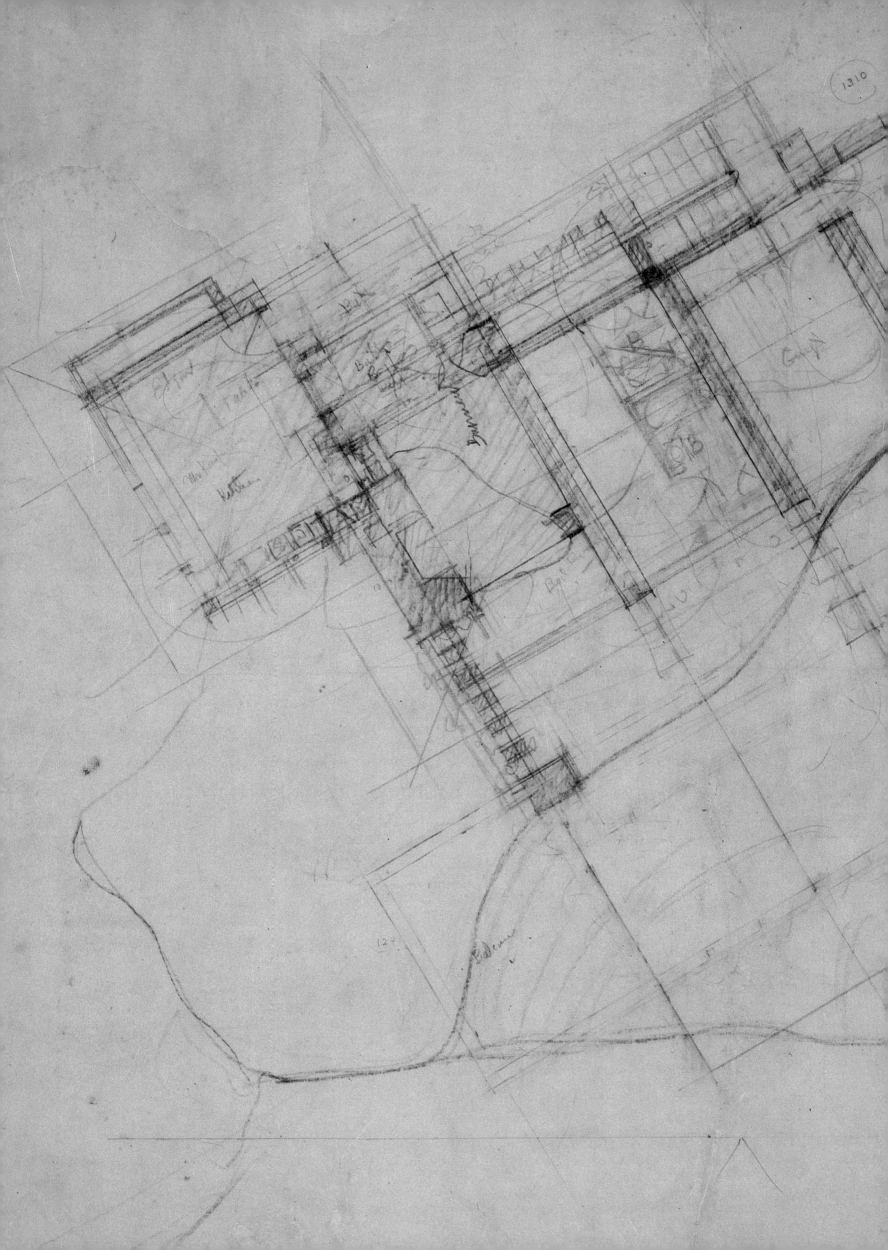

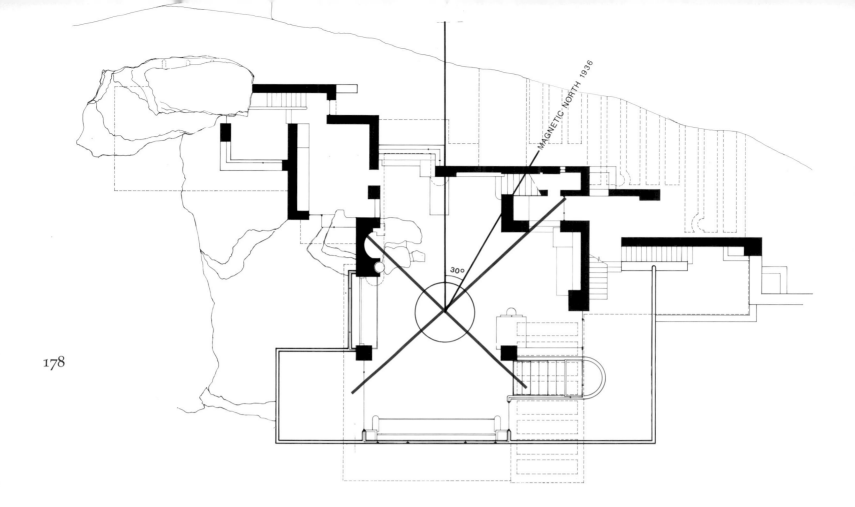

The plan of Fallingwater shows that Frank Lloyd Wright used three separate organizing devices, uniting them in his great design.

Orientation enabled him to set the building firmly into the complex terrain and assured favorable exposures to daylight and weather.

Orthogonal cantilevering extended broadly in serene repose while providing spaces amenable to the habits of the clients and forms responsive to the natural features of the site.

A contrasting diagonal pattern evoked hospitality as it led from the entry across the open living room to the balcony above the falls; then, reaching from the hearthstone to the hatchway over the stream, it recalled ancient cosmic elements—earth and fire, air and water.

The union of these devices culminated at the center of the big room where the axes of all three cross each other in immaterial accord.

Moreover, façades end; their statement is fixed. But structures set at an angle cause the observer to go around corners, exploring, moving on. Architecture becomes dynamic.

Diagonality was explored by Wright over the years, as has been demonstrated by various scholars. Diagonal layouts of a structure, diagonal paths of movement or vistas through buildings—these were physical events. At Fallingwater Wright used diagonality differently. I believe it was the first time he separated virtual paths of signification from material structure, creating a new counterpoint. This freed and clarified central concepts, influencing his later, controversial designs. Wright has rung changes on expectations, stirring people out of their habituations but not depriving them of comforts; he made Fallingwater exciting but not disturbing.

Fallingwater thus reveals the astonishing vitality of Wright's architecture, which he endows with riches like those of polyphonic music, stirring responses instinctual as well as rational and esthetic. Through this human wholeness the architecture of Frank Lloyd Wright appears unique in the twentieth century.

AFTERWORD

Fallingwater's Future

No one has been close to Fallingwater for so long a time as I have. I can testify to the freshness and delight that pervade the house and its setting. The house transformed its setting and, united, they became a symbol of twentieth-century creativity. But Fallingwater is more than a symbol; it has participated, and still does, in living experiences; it must be seen as a focus of change! The very name, Fallingwater, coined by Wright, suggests continuing change. His work on Bear Run welcomes changes of weather and seasons, of nature outside and human nature within; it has changed from private to public occupation. Inevitably more changes will come, beyond present imagining. Is it possible to elicit an essential Fallingwater, an element that survived change and will continue to do so? It would be a dynamic process, for the waterfall is a process, like the impact of the architecture above it, or the lives of those who dwelt in it or who visit it. Components of a basic process have been assembling for a good while. Agelong upheavals of Earth formed the natural terrain, and the terrain nourished life. Humans came—aborigines, settlers, vacationers—among the last my family. The family called on genius, and the terrain—barely altered—gained deep significance. This attracted fame, and fame summoned visitors, entailing the Conservancy. Thus it is clear that the dynamic process at the core of Fallingwater is *a necessary unifying of humankind and the natural environment.* When this is appreciated, Fallingwater is understood and will continue to be adaptive, "opening the mind of human beings . . . to a sense of the marvelous."

ACKNOWLEDGMENTS

Many people have helped me to appreciate and understand Fallingwater; more than can be named here: friends, colleagues, associates, teachers, and, not least, students. Ralph H. Demmler, among the trustees of the Edgar J. Kaufmann Foundation, was especially assiduous in bringing Fallingwater into the public domain. Special gratitude is due also to Thomas M. Schmidt of the Western Pennsylvania Conservancy; for years, among a host of other duties, he has guided Fallingwater with acumen and devotion. Walton Rawls, as editor, ably strengthened both text and illustrations. Archives have generously assisted, particularly those of the Frank Lloyd Wright Memorial Foundation, Avery Memorial Library at Columbia University, the Museum of Modern Art, New York, and the Museum of Art, Carnegie Institute, Pittsburgh. For personal support and guidance I gladly thank W. F. P. and P. M. D.

E. K., jr.

BIBLIOGRAPHY

Prepared by Robert L. Sweeney

1937

Brownell, Baker, and Frank Lloyd Wright. *Architecture and Modern Life*. New York and London: Harper & Brothers Publishers, 1937. Facing p. 86. Construction photographs.

1938

New York. Museum of Modern Art. *A New House by Frank Lloyd Wright on Bear Run, Pennsylvania*. New York: Museum of Modern Art, 1938. Photo study, published in conjunction with an exhibition of photographs of "Fallingwater." It includes a statement by Wright.

"Art." *Time* XXXI (21 February 1938), p. 53.

"Fallingwater, een landhuis van Frank Lloyd Wright." *Bouwkundig Weekblad Architectura* LIX (23 April 1938), pp. 137–38.

"Fallingwater: Kaufmann House, Pennsylvania, Frank Lloyd Wright." *Kokusai Kentiku* XIV (April, 1938), pls. 149–56. Reprinted from *Architectural Forum*, January, 1938.

"'Fallingwater,' vivienda en Pensilvania, arq. Frank Lloyd Wright." *Nuestra Arquitectura* (October, 1938), pp. 336–45.

Hamlin, Talbot F. "F.L.W.—An Analysis." *Pencil Points* XIX (March, 1938), pp. 137–44. A condensed version appeared in *Architect's World* I (April, 1938), pp. 159–63.

Mumford, Lewis. "The Skyline—at Home, Indoors and Out." *New Yorker* XIII (12 February 1938), p. 31.

Patterson, Augusta Owen. "Three Modern Houses, No. 3: Owner, Edgar J. Kaufmann, Pittsburgh; Architect, Frank Lloyd Wright." *Town and Country* XCIII (February, 1938), pp. 64–65, 104.

Peterson, Jay. "Nature's Architect." *New Masses* XXVI (8 February 1938), pp. 29–30.

Wright, Frank Lloyd. "Frank Lloyd Wright." *Architectural Forum* LXVIII (January, 1938), pp. 36–47. A special issue, written and designed by Wright, which includes "Fallingwater."

"Wright's Newest." *Art Digest* XII (1 February 1938), p. 13.

1939

Wright, Frank Lloyd. *An Organic Architecture: The Architecture of Democracy*. The Sir George Watson Lectures of the Sulgrave Manor Board for 1939. London: Lund Humphries & Co., 1939, 1970.

1942

Hitchcock, Henry-Russell. *In the Nature of Materials: 1887–1941, the Buildings of Frank Lloyd Wright*. New York: Duell, Sloan and Pearce, 1942, 1973. Pp. 89–92; ills. 320–23, 370–73. British edition, 1958. Pp. [64–68].

1943

Wright, Frank Lloyd. *An Autobiography*. New York: Duell, Sloan and Pearce, 1943. P. 448.

1945

Mock, Elizabeth, editor, and Philip L. Goodwin, Foreword. *Built in USA Since 1932*. New York: The Museum of Modern Art, 1945. Pp. 26–27.

1952

Moser, Werner M. *Frank Lloyd Wright: Sechzig Jahre lebendige Architektur; Sixty Years of Living Architecture*. Winterthur: Verlag Buchdruckerei Winterthur AG., 1952. Pp. 83–85. Includes a statement by Wright.

1955

Hill, John deKoven. "The Poetry of Structure." *House Beautiful* XCVIII (November, 1955), pp. 246–47, 348–50.

1957

Boyd, Robin. "Two Ways with Modern Monuments." *Architects' Journal* CXXV (April, 1957), pp. 523, 525.

"One Hundred Years of Significant Building, 9: Houses Since 1907." *Architectural Record* CXXI (February, 1957), pp. 199–206.

1959

Wright, Frank Lloyd. *Drawings for a Living Architecture*. New York: Published for the Bear Run Foundation Inc. and the Edgar J. Kaufmann Charitable Foundation by Horizon Press, 1959. Pp. 88–93.

1960

Scully, Vincent, Jr. *Frank Lloyd Wright*. New York: George Braziller, Inc., 1960. Pp. 26–27, ills. 72–76.

Wright, Frank Lloyd. *Frank Lloyd Wright: Writings and Buildings*. Selected by Edgar Kaufmann, jr., and Ben Raeburn. New York: Horizon Press, 1960. Pp. 136–37, 272–76. From *Architectural Forum*, January, 1938. South American edition, 1962; German edition, 1963; Japanese edition, 1976.

1962

Wright, Frank Lloyd. *The Drawings of Frank Lloyd Wright*. Selected by Arthur Drexler. New York: Horizon Press for the Museum of Modern Art, 1962. Pls. 137–40, 275. Notes to plates, pp. 303, 315.

"La Casa de la Cascada: historia de una epopeya." *Nuestra Arquitectura* no. 397 (December, 1962), pp. 8, 10.

Kaufmann, Edgar, jr. "Frank Lloyd Wright's Fallingwater 25 Years After." *Architettura* VIII (August, 1962), pp. 222–80. Reprinted in book form in 1963 (below).

Zevi, Bruno. "Il vaticinio del Riegl e la Casa sulla Cascata." *Architettura* VIII (August, 1962), pp. 218–21. Reprinted in book form in 1963 (below).

1963

Zevi, Bruno, and Edgar Kaufmann, jr. *La Casa sulla Cascata di F. Ll. Wright: F. Lloyd Wright's Fallingwater*. Milano, Italy: ET/AS Kompass, 1963.

REVIEW

Kostka, Robert. *Prairie School Review* I, no. 3 (1964), p. 17.

"Fallingwater Saved Before It Is Imperiled: Kaufmann Makes a Gift of House at Bear Run." *Architectural Record* CXXXIV (October, 1963), p. 24.

"Wright Masterpiece Preserved." *Interiors* CXXIII (October, 1963), p. 12.

1964

Engel, Martin. "The Ambiguity of Frank Lloyd Wright: Fallingwater." *Charette* XLIV (April, 1964), pp. 17–18.

"A House of Leaves: The Poetry of Fallingwater." *Charette* XLIV (April, 1964), pp. 13–16.

Lewis, Charles F. "Doors Open at Fallingwater." *Carnegie Magazine* XXXVIII (September, 1964), pp. 237–40.

1966

Smith, Norris Kelly. *Frank Lloyd Wright. A Study in Architectural Content.* Englewood Cliffs, N.J.: Prentice-Hall, Inc., 1966, 1979. Pp. 127–36.

1968

Futagawa, Yukio, photographer, and Tsutomu Ikuta and Hiroshi Misawa, text. *F. Ll. Wright, 2.* Tokyo: Bijutsu Shuppansha, 1968. Pp. 62–69.

1970

Futagawa, Yukio, editor and photographer, and Paul Rudolph, text. *Frank Lloyd Wright: Kaufmann House, "Fallingwater," Bear Run, Pennsylvania, 1936.* Tokyo: A.D.A. Edita, 1970.

1974

Storrer, William Allin. *The Architecture of Frank Lloyd Wright. A Complete Catalogue.* Cambridge, Massachusetts, and London, England: The MIT Press, 1974, 1978. Nos. 230–32.

1975

Lynes, Russell. "On Knowing Wright from Wrong." *Architectural Digest* XXXII (November–December, 1975), pp. 24, 32, 36.

1976

Futagawa, Yukio, editor and photographer. *Houses by Frank Lloyd Wright 2.* Tokyo: A.D.A. Edita, 1976. Pp. 22–29.

Izzo, Alberto and Camillo Gubitosi. *Frank Lloyd Wright: Disegni, 1887–1959.* Firenze: Centro Di, 1976. Pls. 98–101. French and British editions, 1977. American edition, 1981.

Masuda, Akihisa, photographer, and Masami Tanigawa, text. *The World of Frank Lloyd Wright.* Tokyo: Gihodo Publishing Co., Ltd., 1976. Pp. 17–21, 31.

1977

Wright, Frank Lloyd. *Frank Lloyd Wright: Selected Drawings Portfolio.* New York: Horizon Press, 1977. Pl. 23.

1978

Hoffmann, Donald. *Frank Lloyd Wright's Fallingwater. The House and Its History.* With an Introduction by Edgar Kaufmann, jr. New York: Dover Publications, Inc., 1978.

REVIEWS

Anonymous. *Booklist* LXXV (1 March 1979), p. 1041.

Anonymous. *Progressive Architecture* LX (March, 1979), p. 110.

Atkinson, Fello. "The Wright Solution." *Architects' Journal* CLXIX (18 April 1979), p. 794.

Condit, Carl W. *Technology & Culture* XX (July, 1979), pp. 647–49.

Connors, Joseph. *Journal of the Society of Architectural Historians* XXXVIII (December, 1979), pp. 397–98.

Filler, Martin. "Writing on Wright." *Art in America* LXVII (October, 1979), pp. 77–79.

Sergeant, John. "Three Wrights." *Architectural Review* CLXVI (October, 1979), p. 204.

Tafel, Edgar. *AIA Journal* LXVIII (June, 1979), pp. 81, 84.

Tafel, Edgar. *Frank Lloyd Wright Newsletter* I, no. 6 (November–December, 1978), p. 11.

Blanc, Alan. "Forty Years on: Fallingwater, Frank Lloyd Wright's Most Famous House." *Building Design* no. 399 (9 June 1978), p. 24.

"Fallingwater Feedback." *Progressive Architecture* LIX (July, 1978), p. 10.

Gueft, Olga. "In the Forest on the Way to Bear Run." *Contract Interiors* CXXXVII (May, 1978), pp. 150–51.

"Public Buildings in the East." *Frank Lloyd Wright Newsletter* I, no. 3 (May–June, 1978), p. 3.

1979

Hanks, David A. *The Decorative Designs of Frank Lloyd Wright.* New York: E. P. Dutton, 1979. Pp. 145–47, 152, 205.

Tafel, Edgar. *Apprentice to Genius.* Years with Frank Lloyd Wright. New York: McGraw-Hill Book Company, 1979. Pp. 3–9, 85, 121, 174–75. German edition, 1981. Paperback edition, 1985.

1980

Arts Council of Great Britain. *10 Twentieth Century Houses.* Exhibition Compiled and Written by John Miller. 1980. Pp. 16–17.

Hoesli, Bernhard. "Frank Lloyd Wright: Falling Water." *A+U* no. 118 (July, 1980), pp. 155–66.

1981

Abercrombie, Stanley. "When a House Becomes a Museum." *AIA Journal* LXX (August, 1981), pp. 54–57.

"Frank Lloyd Wright." *A+U* no. 7 (1981), pp. 151–57.

"New Visitors Center Completed at Fallingwater." *Frank Lloyd Wright Newsletter* IV, no. 2 (Second Quarter, 1981), p. 18.

1982

Heinz, Thomas A. *Frank Lloyd Wright.* New York: St. Martin's Press, 1982. Pp. 70–71.

Levine, Neil. "Frank Lloyd Wright's Diagonal Planning." In *In Search of Modern Architecture. A Tribute to Henry-Russell Hitchcock.* New York: The Architectural History Foundation, and Cambridge, Massachusetts, and London, England: The MIT Press, 1982. Pp. 265, 267–68.

Netting, M. Graham. "Fallingwater & Bear Run." In *50 Years of the Western Pennsylvania Conservancy. The Early Years* by M. Graham Netting. Pittsburgh: The Western Pennsylvania Conservancy, 1982. Pp. 23–29.

Wright, Frank Lloyd. *Letters to Apprentices.* Selected and with Commentary by Bruce Brooks Pfeiffer. Fresno: The Press at California State University, Fresno, 1982. Pp. 116–17, 130–31, 134–35.

"Fallingwater Forum Reunites Three Taliesin Apprentices." *AIA Journal* LXXI (November, 1982), p. 26.

1984

Frank Lloyd Wright Drawings. Tokyo: GA Gallery, 1984. Pl. 19.

Futagawa, Yukio, editor, and Bruce Brooks Pfeiffer, text. *Frank Lloyd Wright in His Renderings 1887–1959.* Tokyo: A.D.A. Edita, 1984. Pl. 98.

1985

Doremus, Thomas. *Frank Lloyd Wright and Le Corbusier. The Great Dialogue.* New York: Van Nostrand Reinhold Company, 1985. Pp. 26–36.

Futagawa, Yukio, editor and photographer, and Bruce Brooks Pfeiffer, text. *Frank Lloyd Wright Monograph 1924–1936.* Tokyo: A.D.A. Edita, 1985. Pls. 266–311.

1986

Wright, Frank Lloyd. *Letters to Clients.* Selected and with Commentary by Bruce Brooks Pfeiffer. Fresno, California: The Press at California State University Press, Fresno, 1986. Pp. 82–109.

INDEX

PHOTOGRAPHY CREDITS

Adirondack Museum, 20 *bottom*, 21 *top* (Richard J. Linke); Art Institute of Chicago, 13 *detail*, 22; L. D. Astorino & Associates, Ltd., Architects, Pittsburgh, 51, 52–53, 73, 90 *left*, 91–95, 97, 109, 117 *bottom*, 128 *top*, 134, 135, 156 *top left*, 178; Avery Library, Columbia University, 35 *bottom*, 44, 45, 48, 50 *top and bottom*, 63 (Thomas M. Martin), 125 *top right*; Carnegie Institute Museum, 34, 54 *top and bottom*, 55 *bottom* (Luke Swank Collection); *Country Life*, 16 *bottom*, 17 *bottom*, 18; Dove Cottage, Grasmere, 14; Oberto Gili, *House & Garden*, 145, 146–47, 152–53; Mark Girouard, 20 *top*; Hedrich-Blessing, 38 *top*, 56, 57, 61, 111, 119 *top*, 123 *top*, 127 *bottom right*; Thomas A. Heinz, 2, 24, 27, 33, 71, 80–81, 98, 101 *right*, 106–7, 112–13, 116–17, 116 *bottom*, 121 *top and bottom*, 138–39, 144 *bottom*, 155, 157, 160 *top left*, 166–67, 173 *bottom*, 181, 182,

184–85; Harvey H. Kaiser, 21 *bottom*; Edgar Kaufmann, jr., 28 *bottom, left and right*, 35 *top, left and right*, 55 *top*; Christopher Little, endpapers, 1, 4, 6, 8, 9, 30, 64, 74, 76, 77, 78 *bottom*, 78–79, 79 *bottom*, 80 *left*, 81 *right*, 82, 84–85, 86 *top and bottom*, 87, 89, 90 *bottom*, 99, 100, 113 *right*, 118 *bottom*, 120, 132–33, 136, 136–37, 140–41, 142, 143 *top and bottom*, 148 *left*, 148–49, 149 *right*, 150–51, 154 *top and bottom*, 156 *top, center, and bottom*, 158–59, 160 *bottom left*, 160–61, 162 *left, top and bottom*, 162–63, 164–65, 169, 171, 172, 173 *top*, 174, 175, 179, 186; Paul Mayén, 69 *top*, 70 *bottom*, 122, 129 *bottom right*; John Mitchell and Sons, 17 *top*; Museum of Modern Art, New York, 28; National Trust for Scotland, 16 *top*; New York Public Library, 20 *center*, 21 *center*; Ada Rodriguez, 102 *top*; Sotheby's, 19; Edgar Tafel, 28 *top right*, 38 *bottom*

(John H. Howe); Time, Inc., 28; Western Pennsylvania Conservancy, 29, 44 *left*, 69 *bottom*, 70, 104, 108, 118 *top*, 119 *bottom*, 123 *center*, 125 *top left*, 129 *top right*, (W. Galen Barton: 59, 103, 110 *top*, 115, 127 *top right*, 128 *bottom*, 130 *top and bottom left*), (Harold Corsini: 58, 62, 114 *top and bottom*, 123 *bottom*, 126, 127 *bottom left*, 129 *bottom left*, 130 *bottom right*, 131 *top and bottom*), (Michael Fedison: 68), (Donald Hoffmann: 36 *top and bottom*, 49, 110 *bottom*), (Paul Mayén: 70 *bottom*, 122, 129 *bottom right*), (Samuel E. Stewart: 31, 37, 125 *bottom*), (Lynda Waggoner: 108 *bottom right*); © Frank Lloyd Wright Foundation, courtesy of the Frank Lloyd Wright Memorial Foundation, 39, 40 *top and bottom*, 41, 42–43, 46, 47, 60 *top and bottom*, 105, 176–77.